This coloring book belongs to:

....

....

....

....

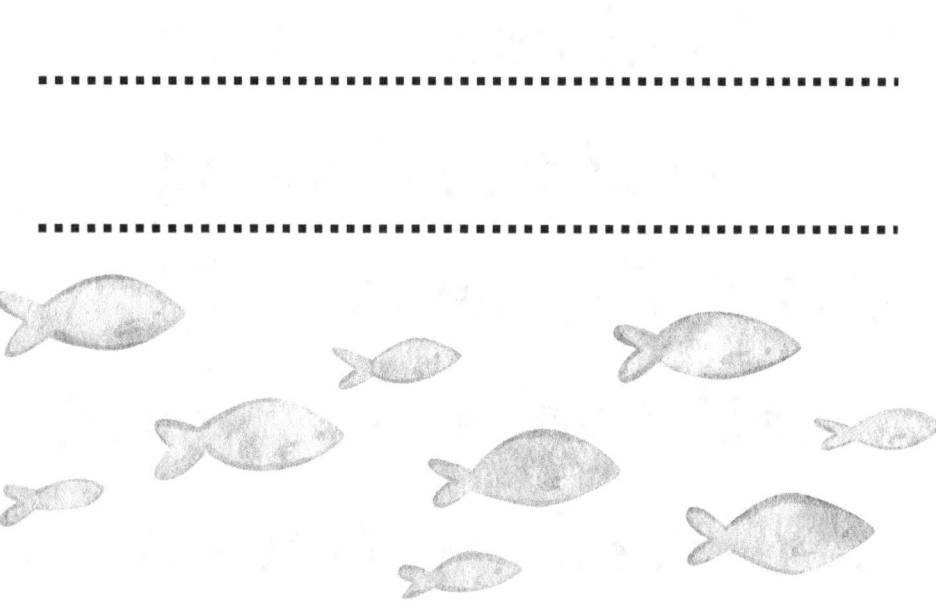

Book created by J.N.

"This image was generated using ChatGPT, an artificial intelligence assistant provided by OpenAI."

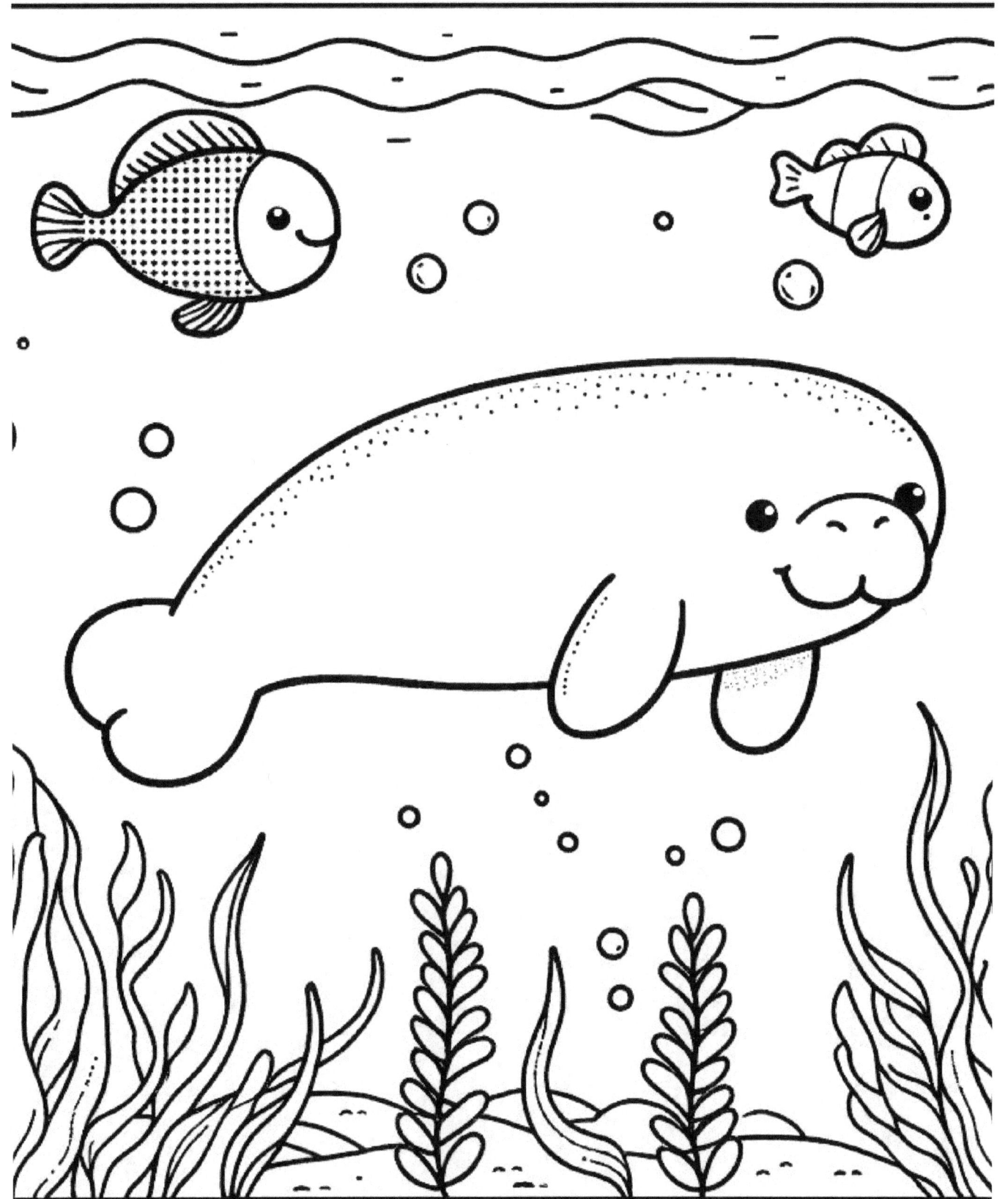

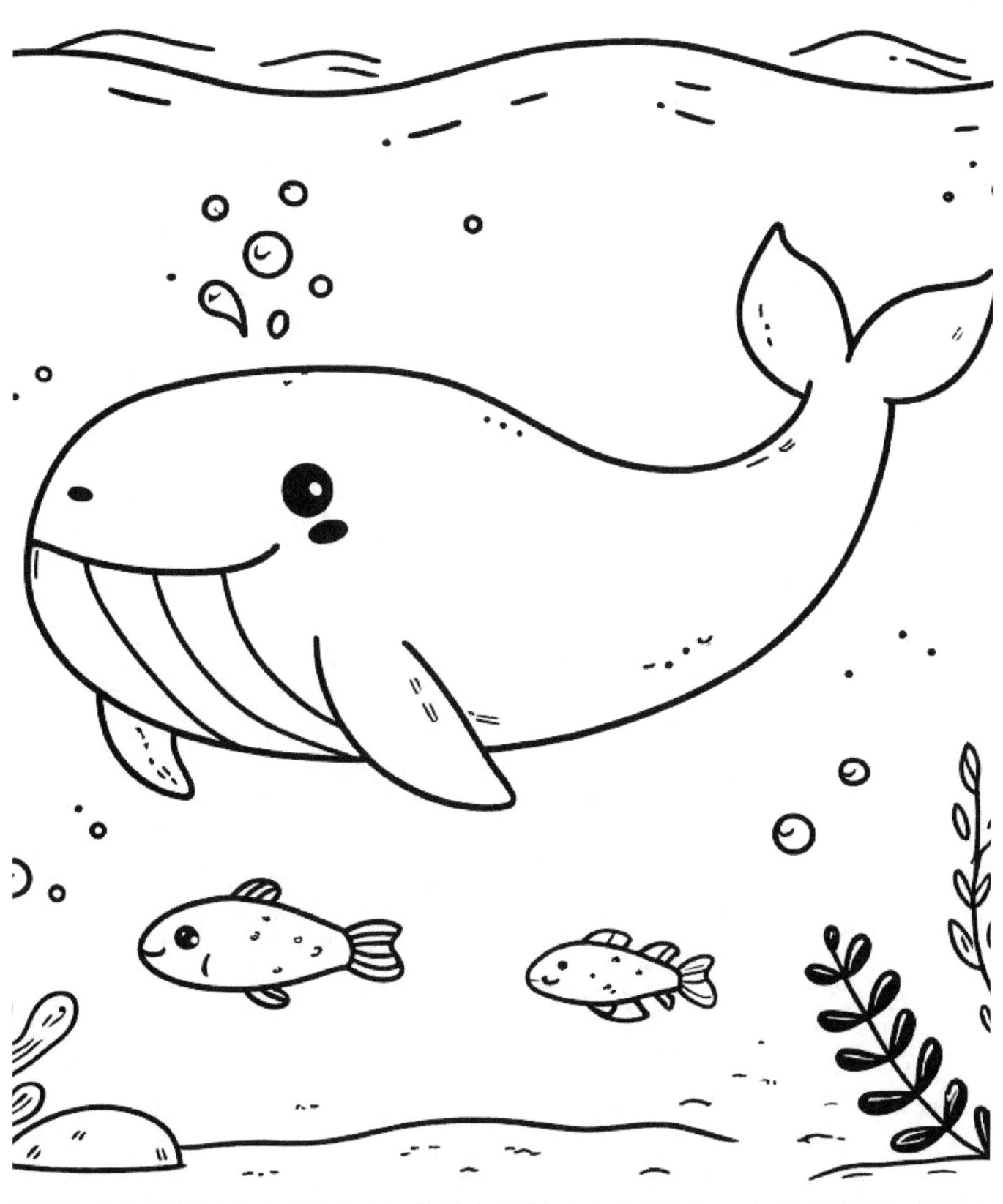

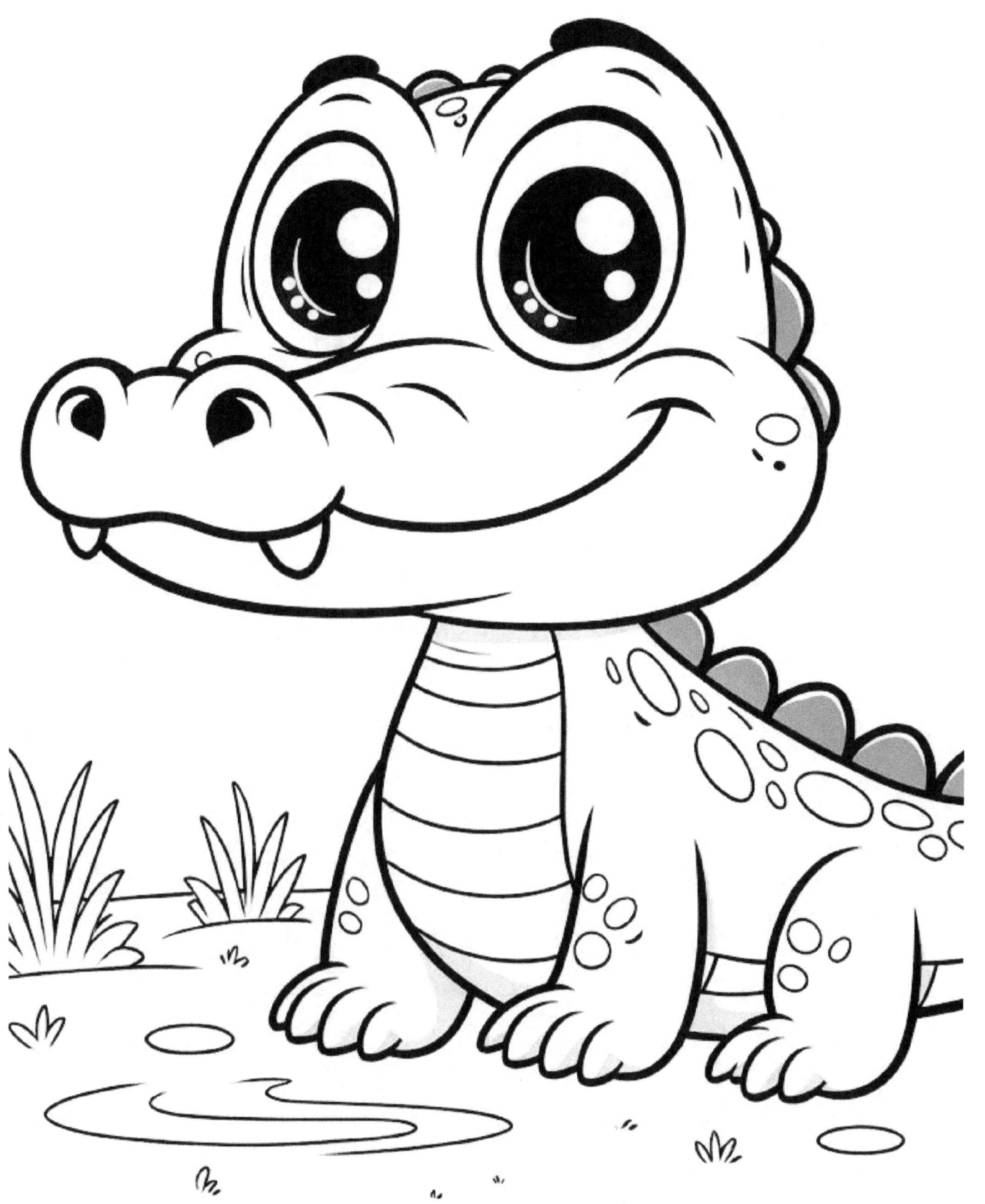

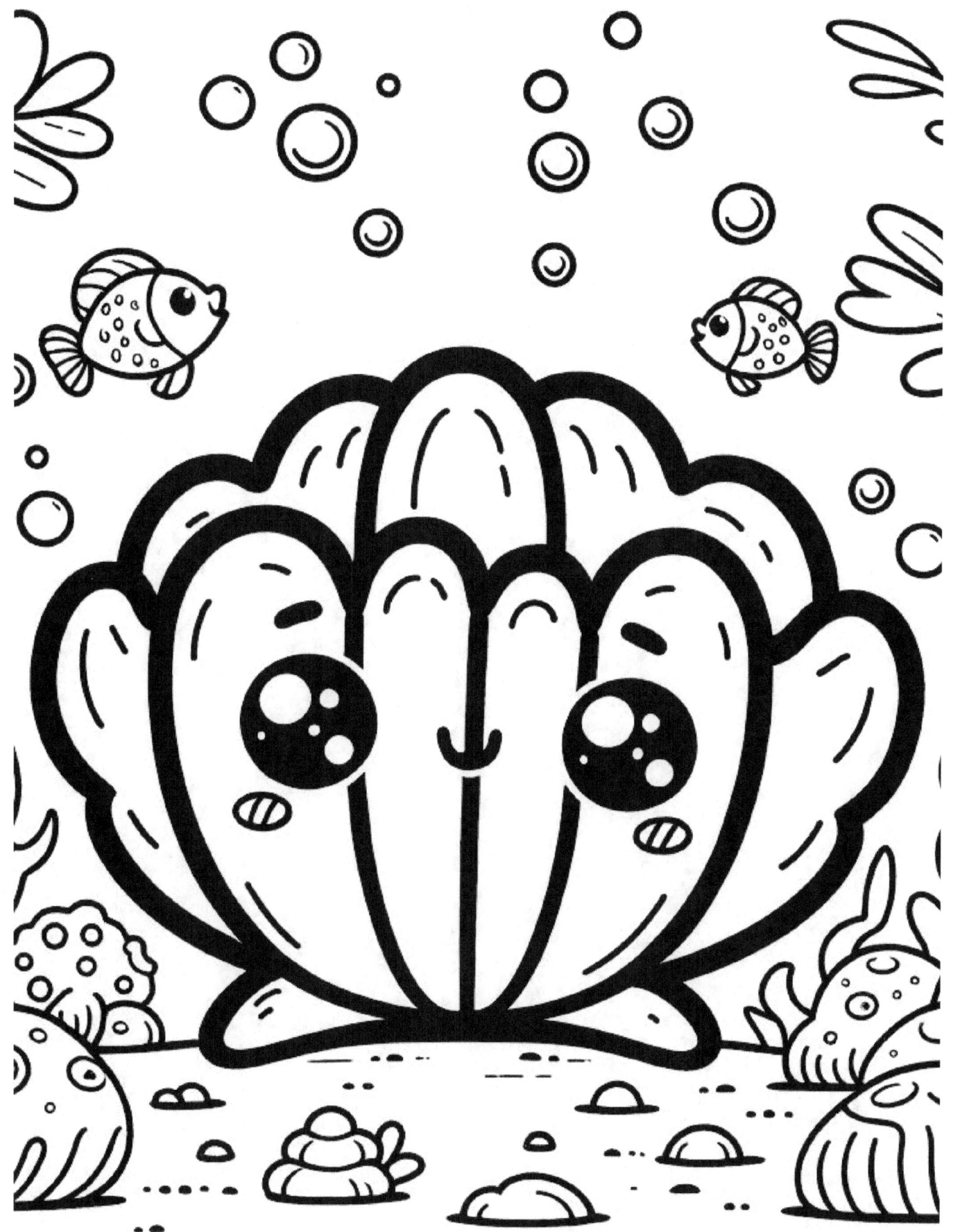

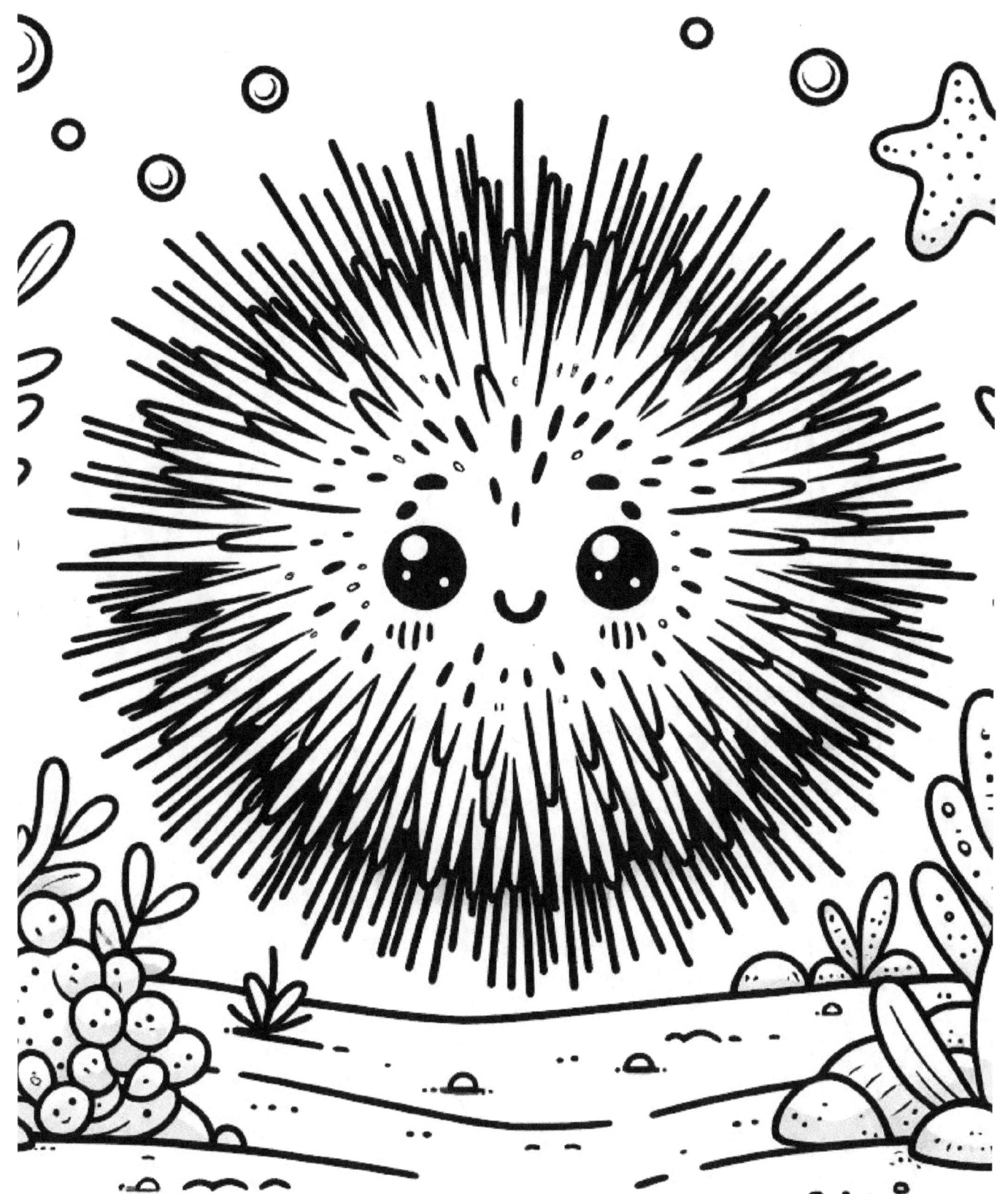

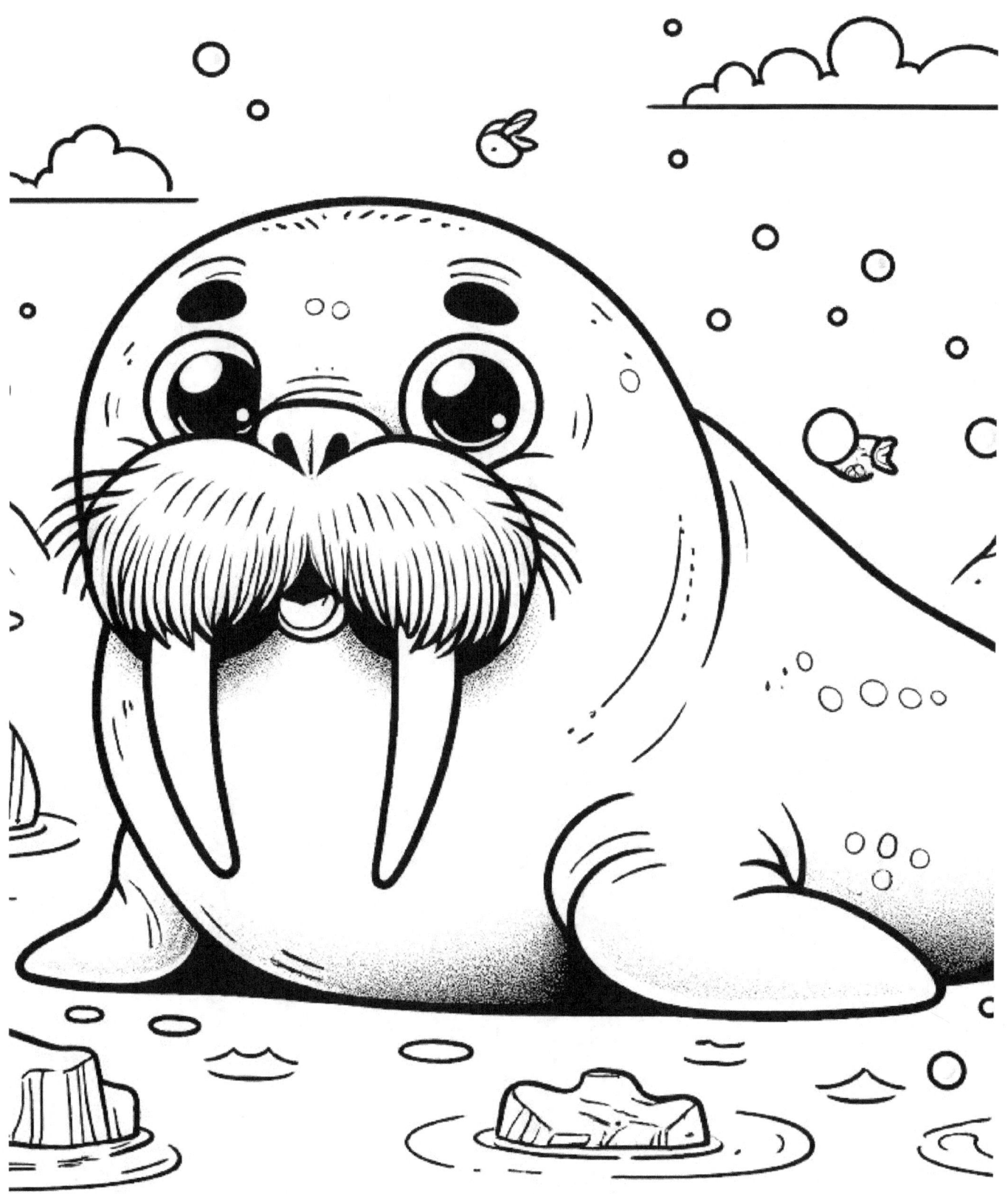

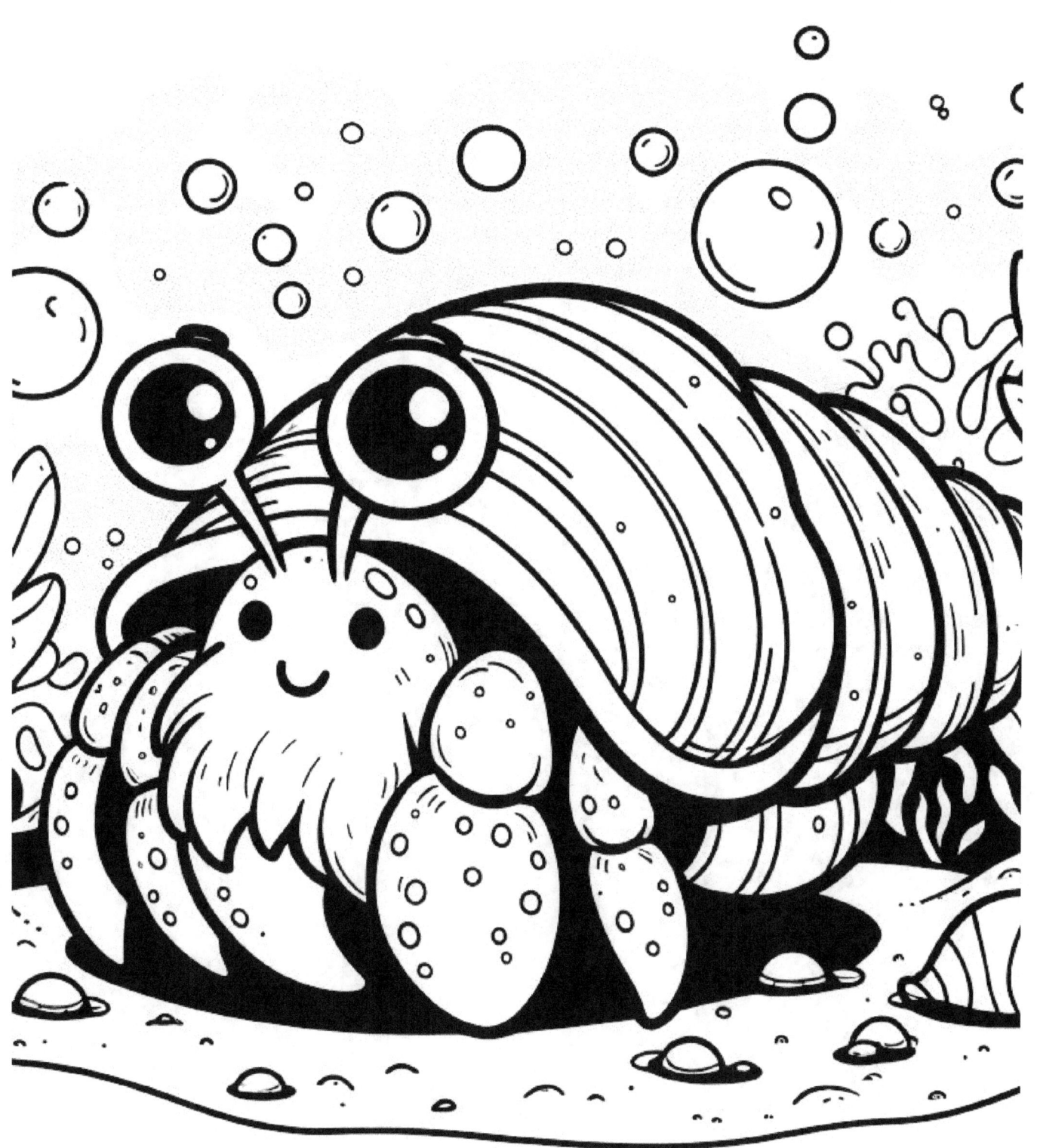

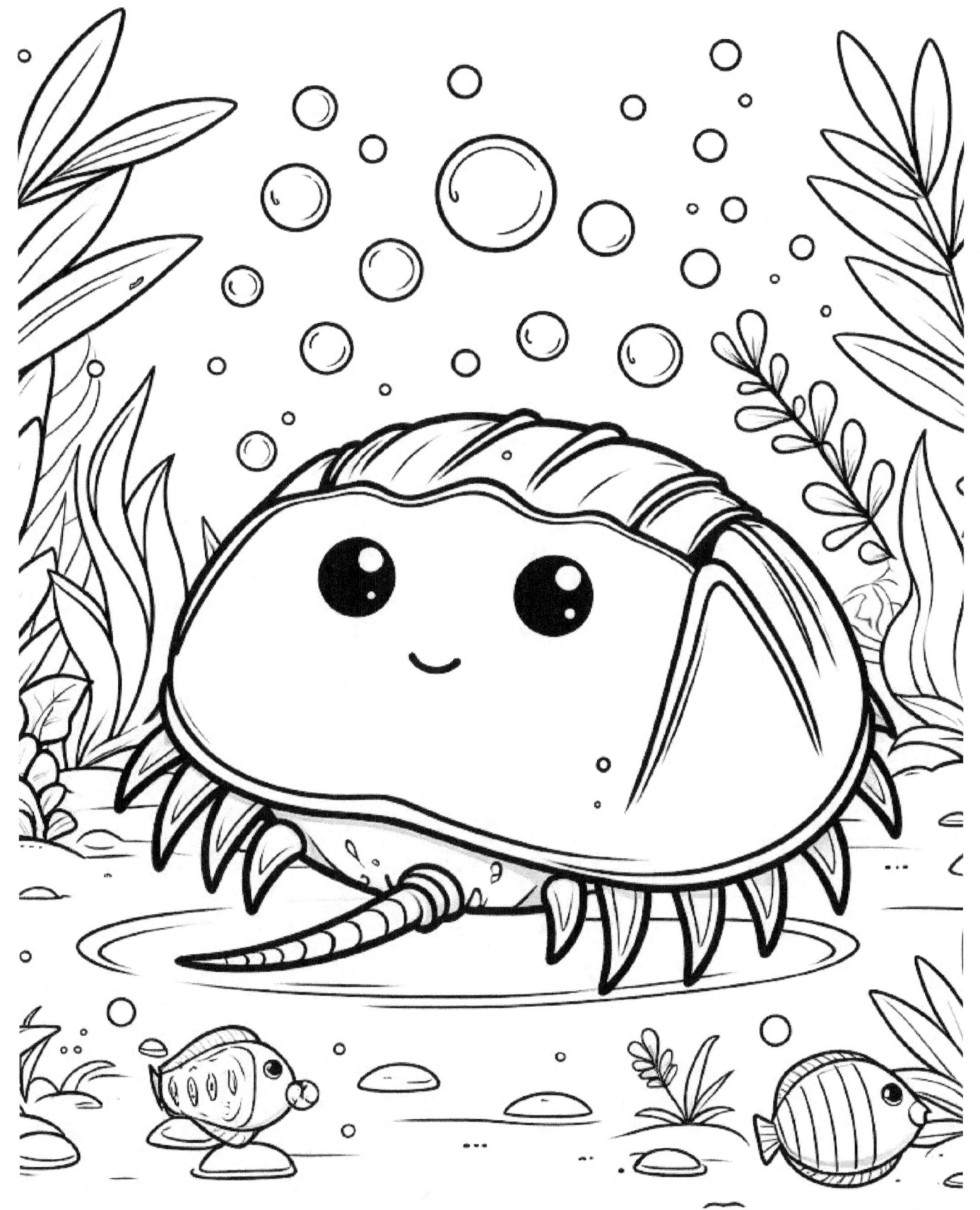

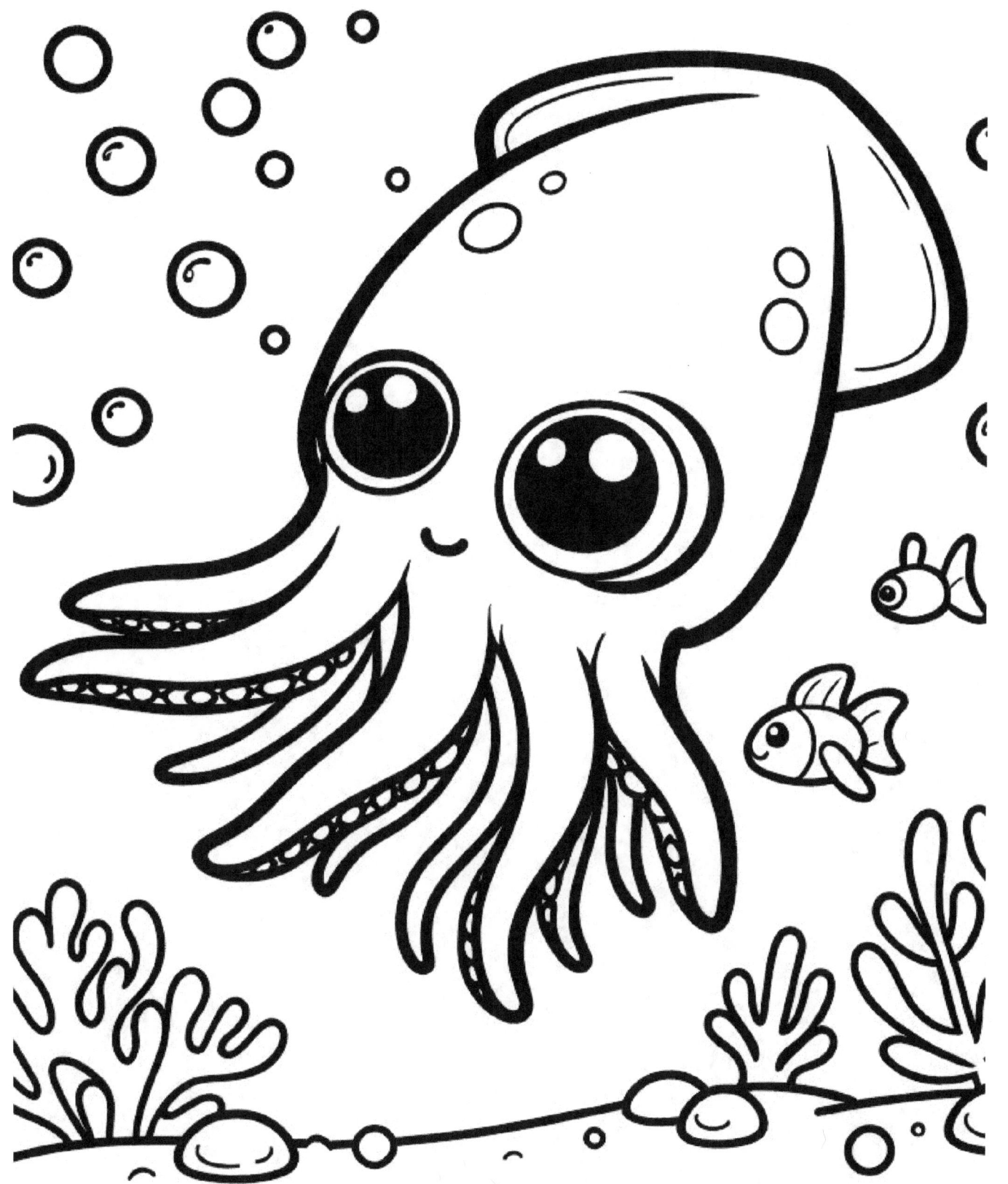

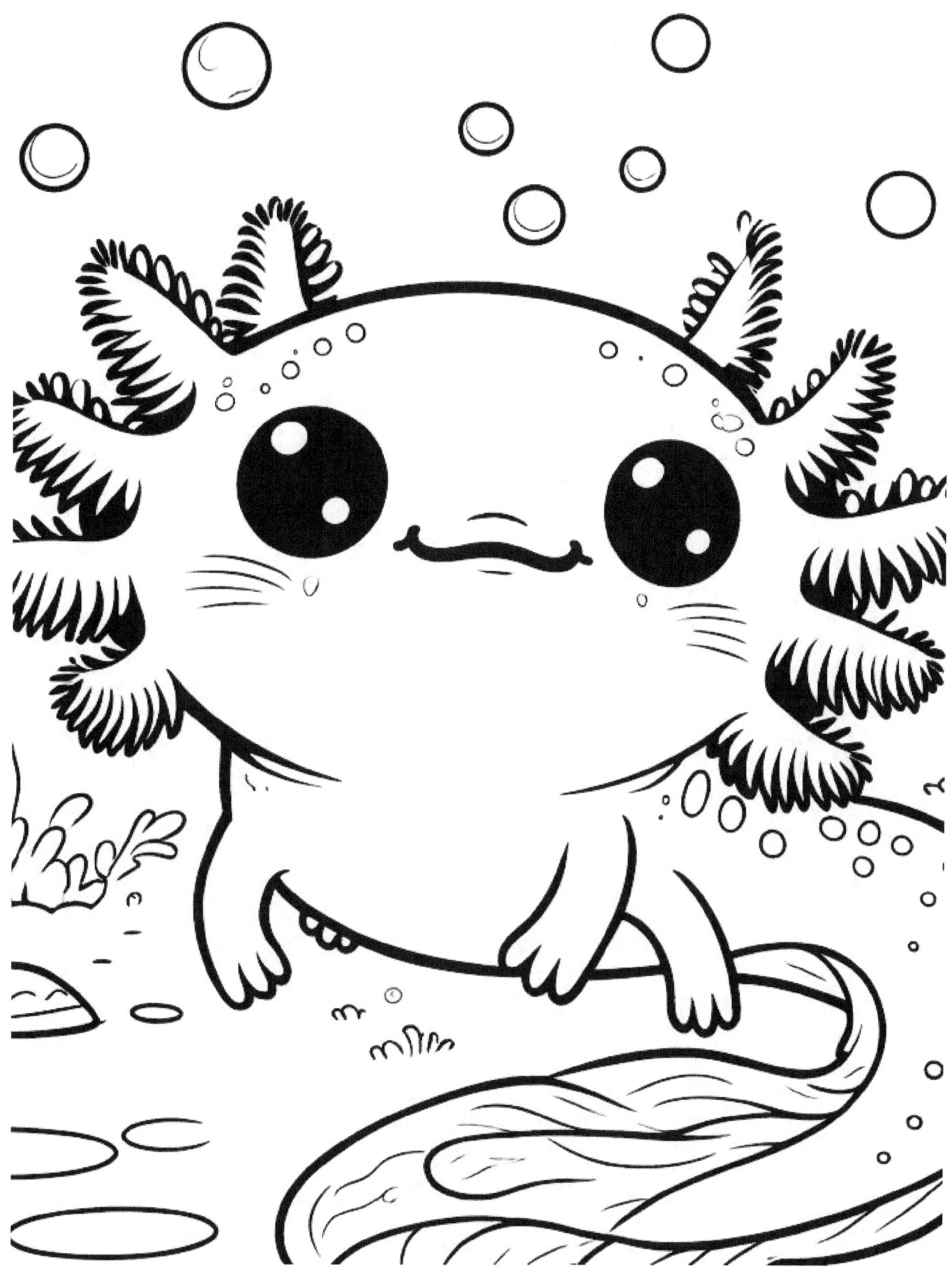

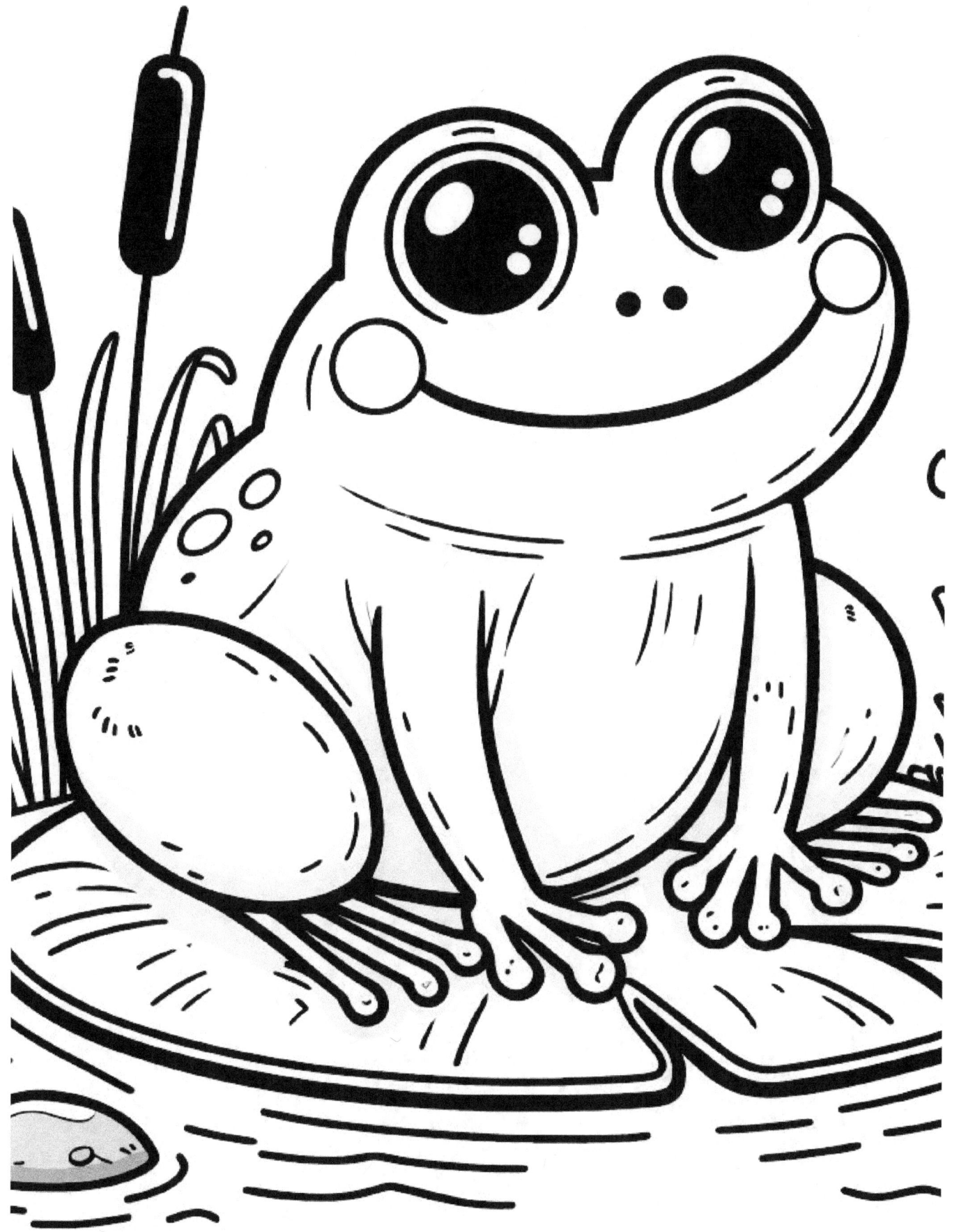

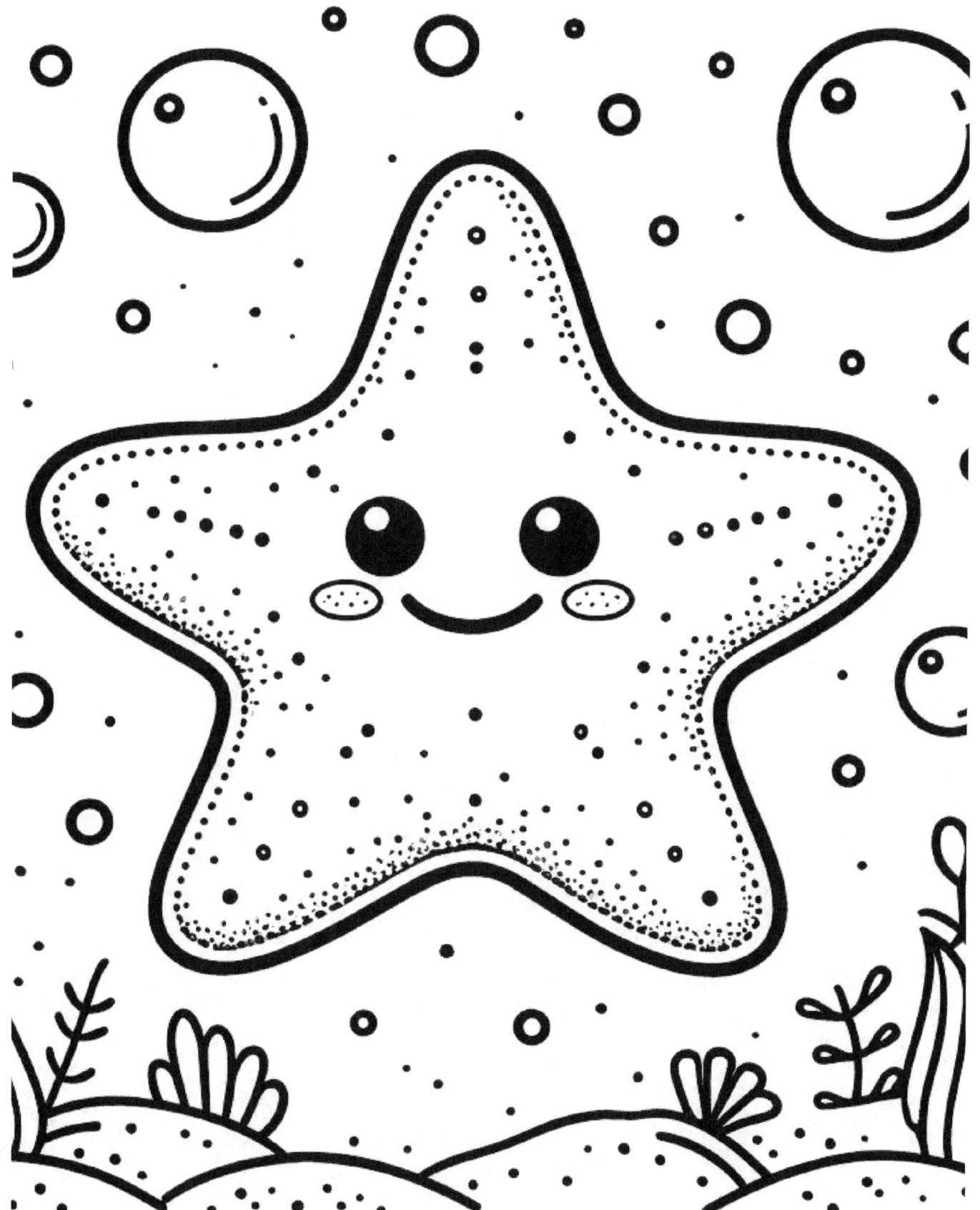

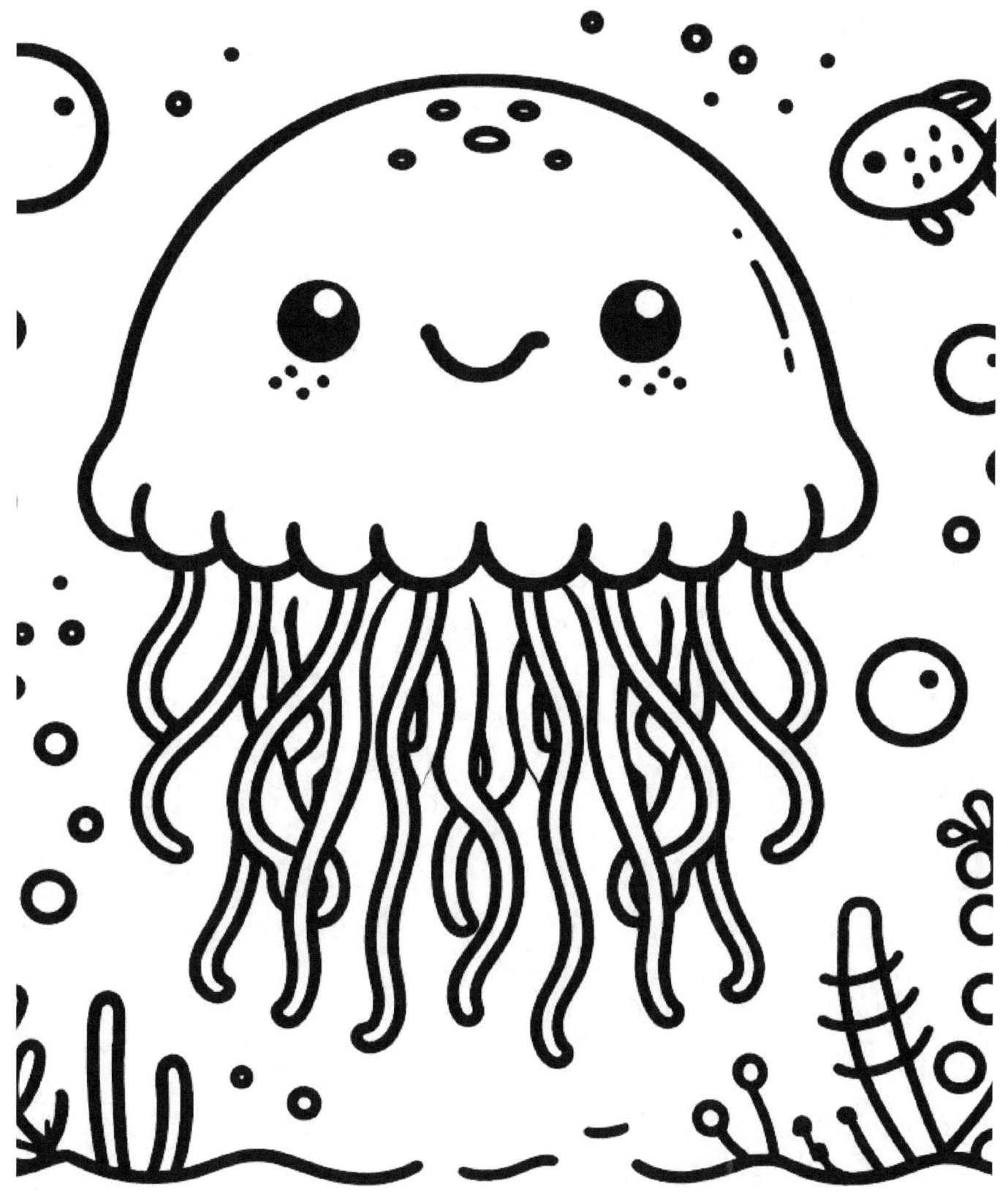

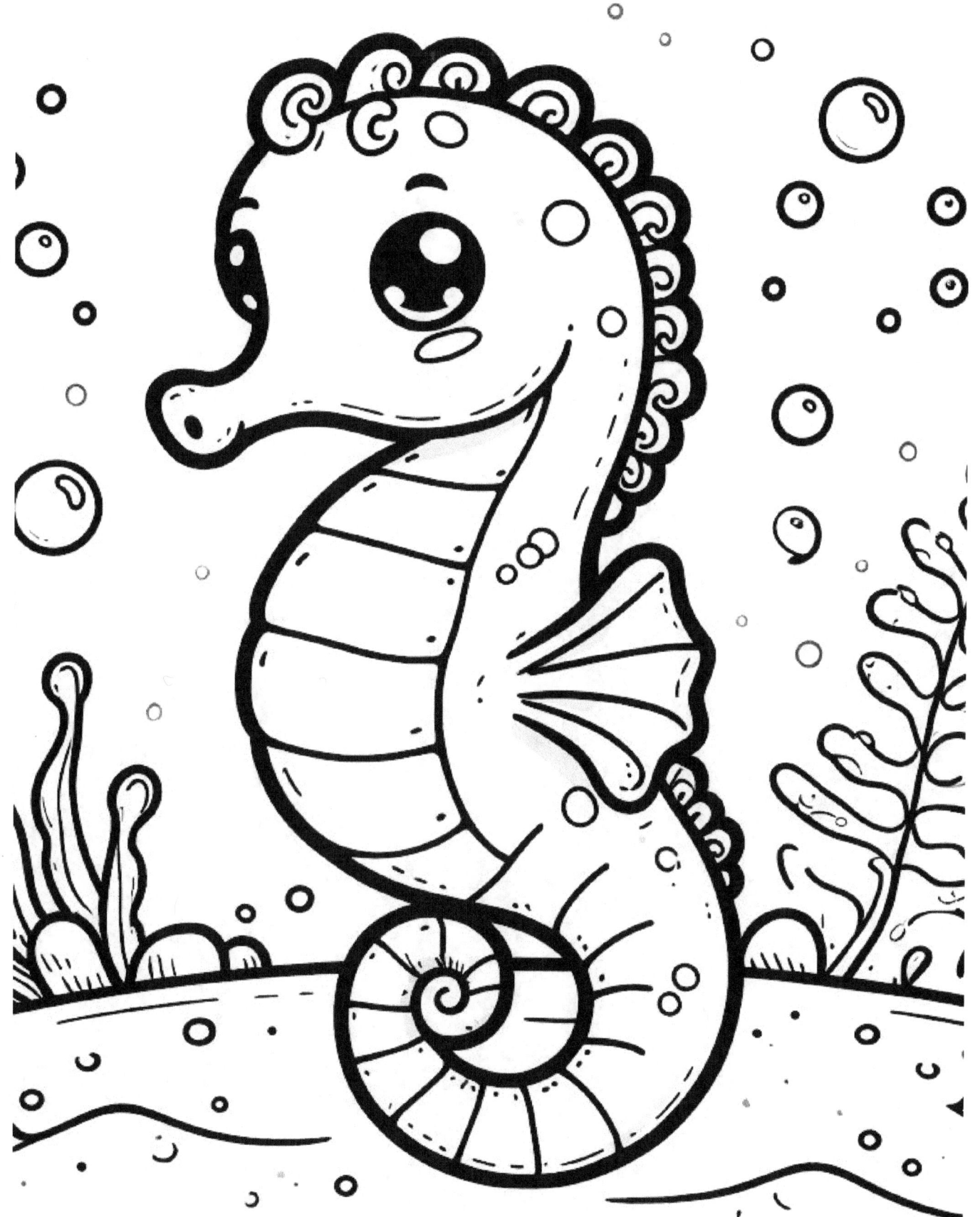

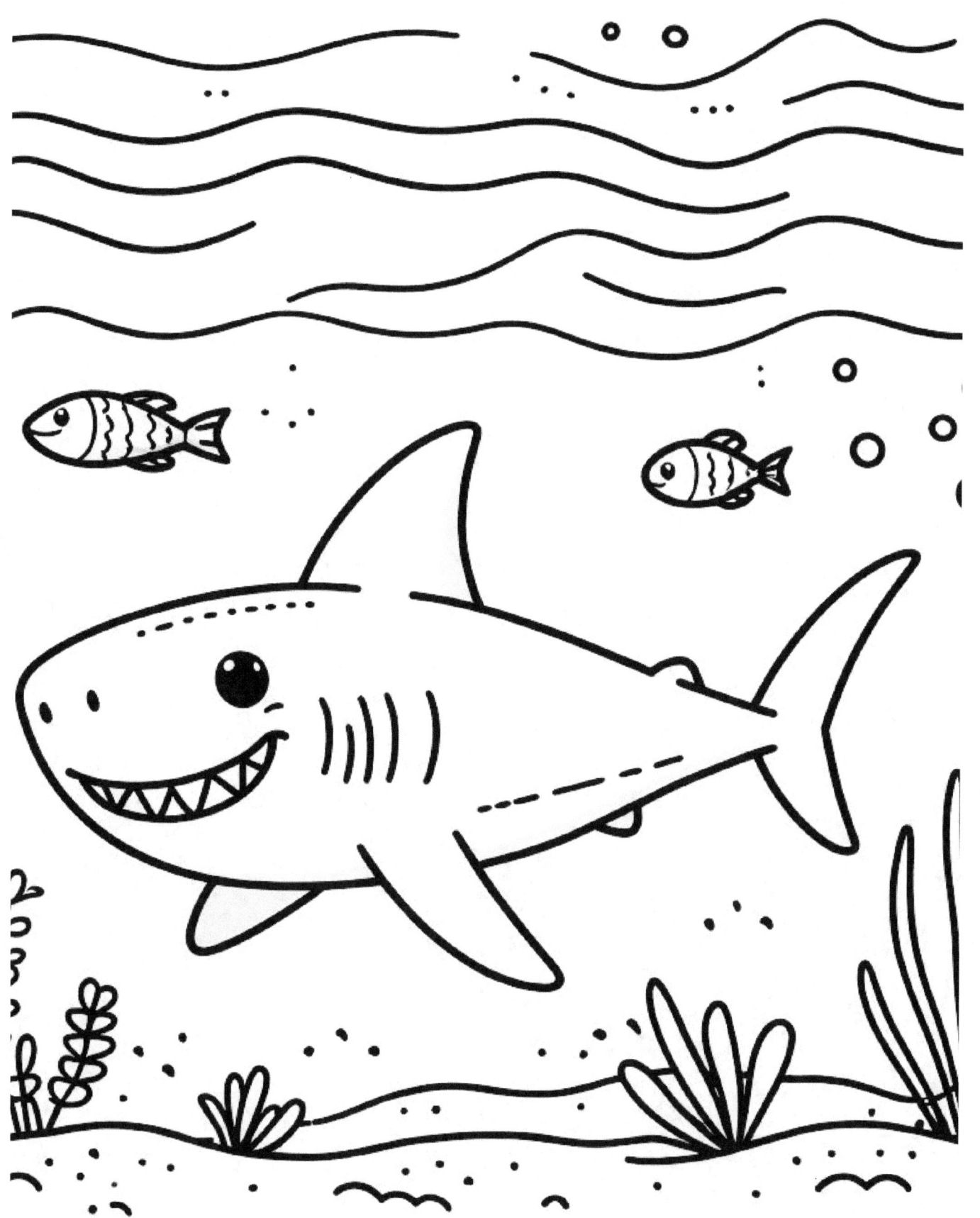

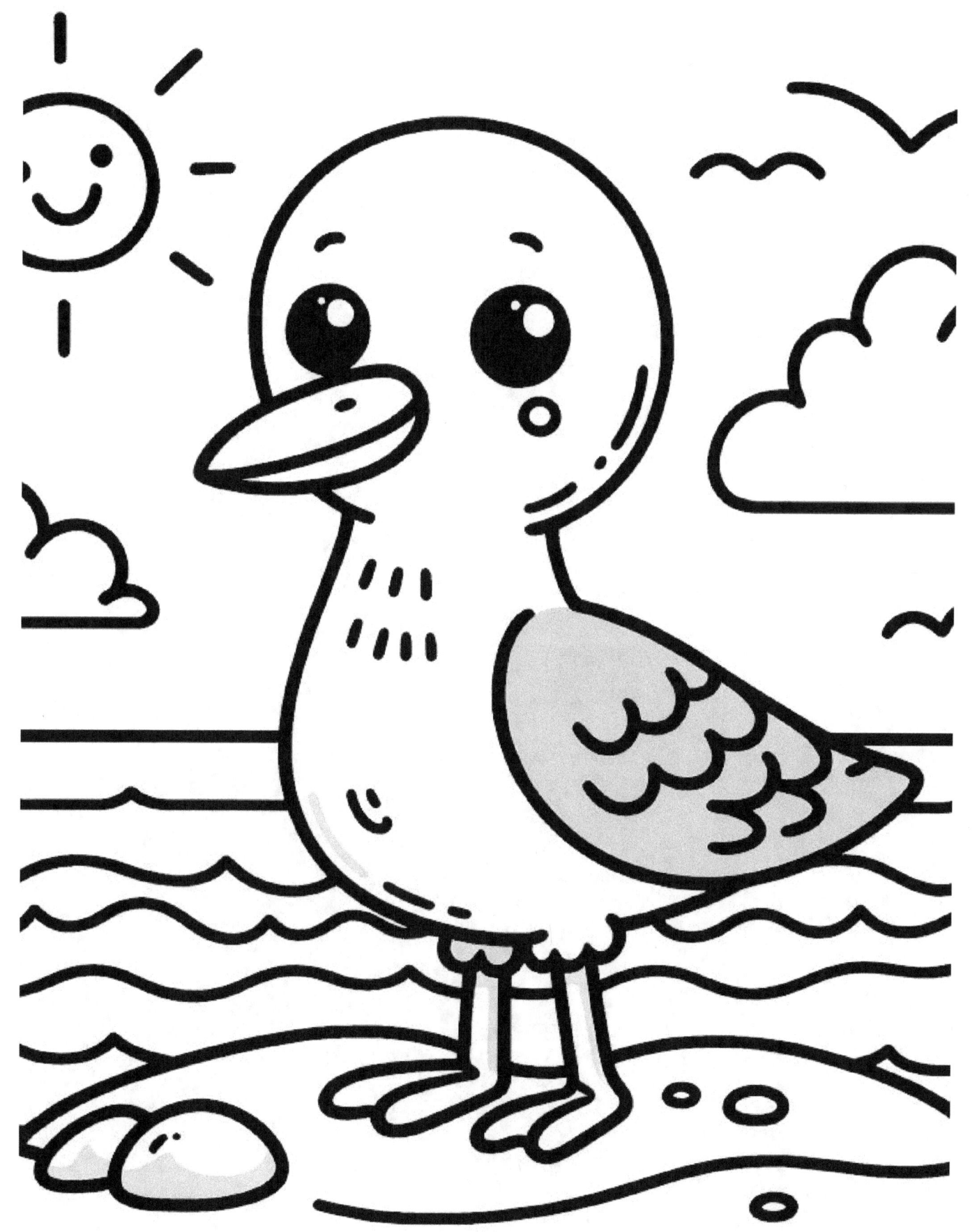

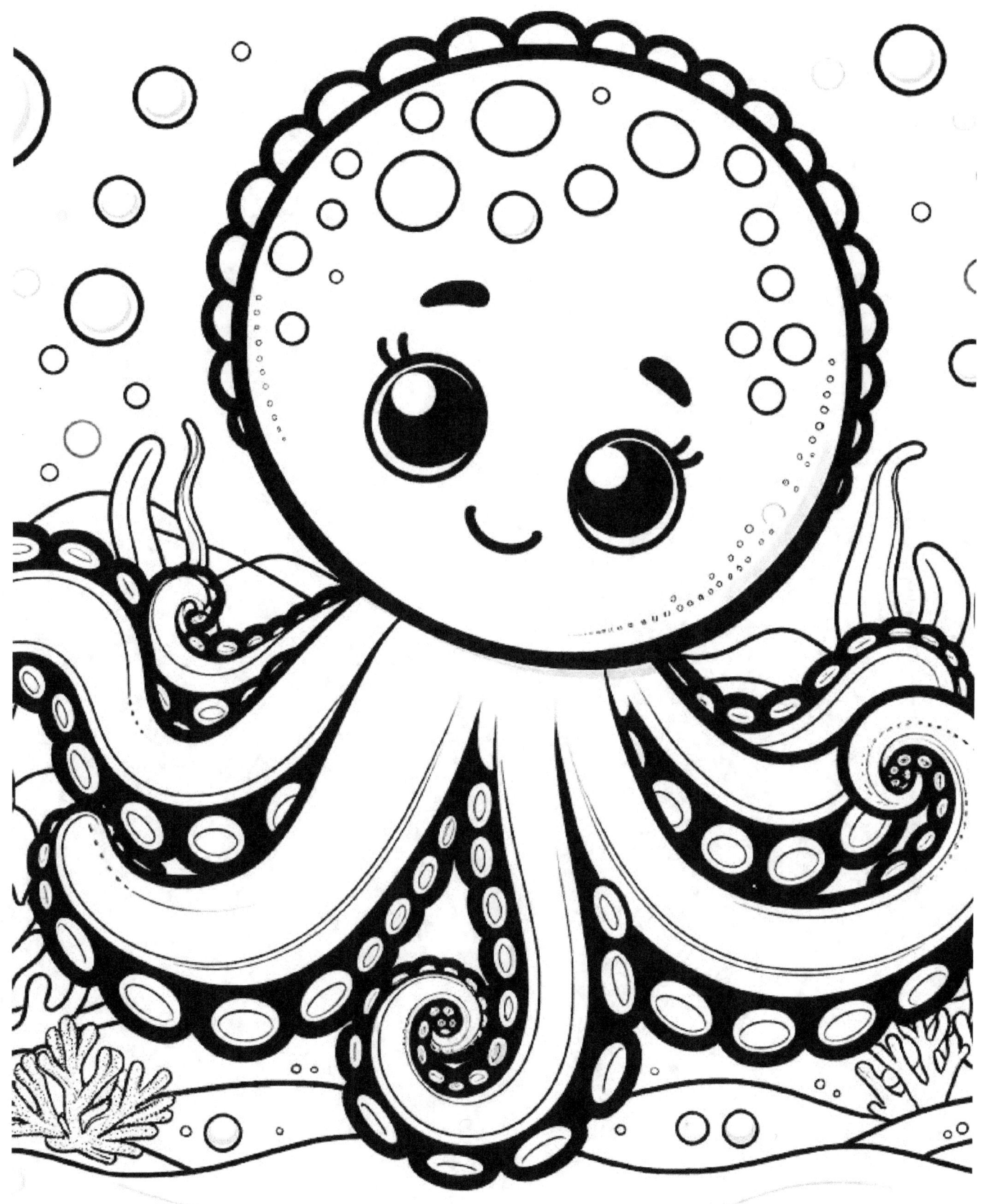

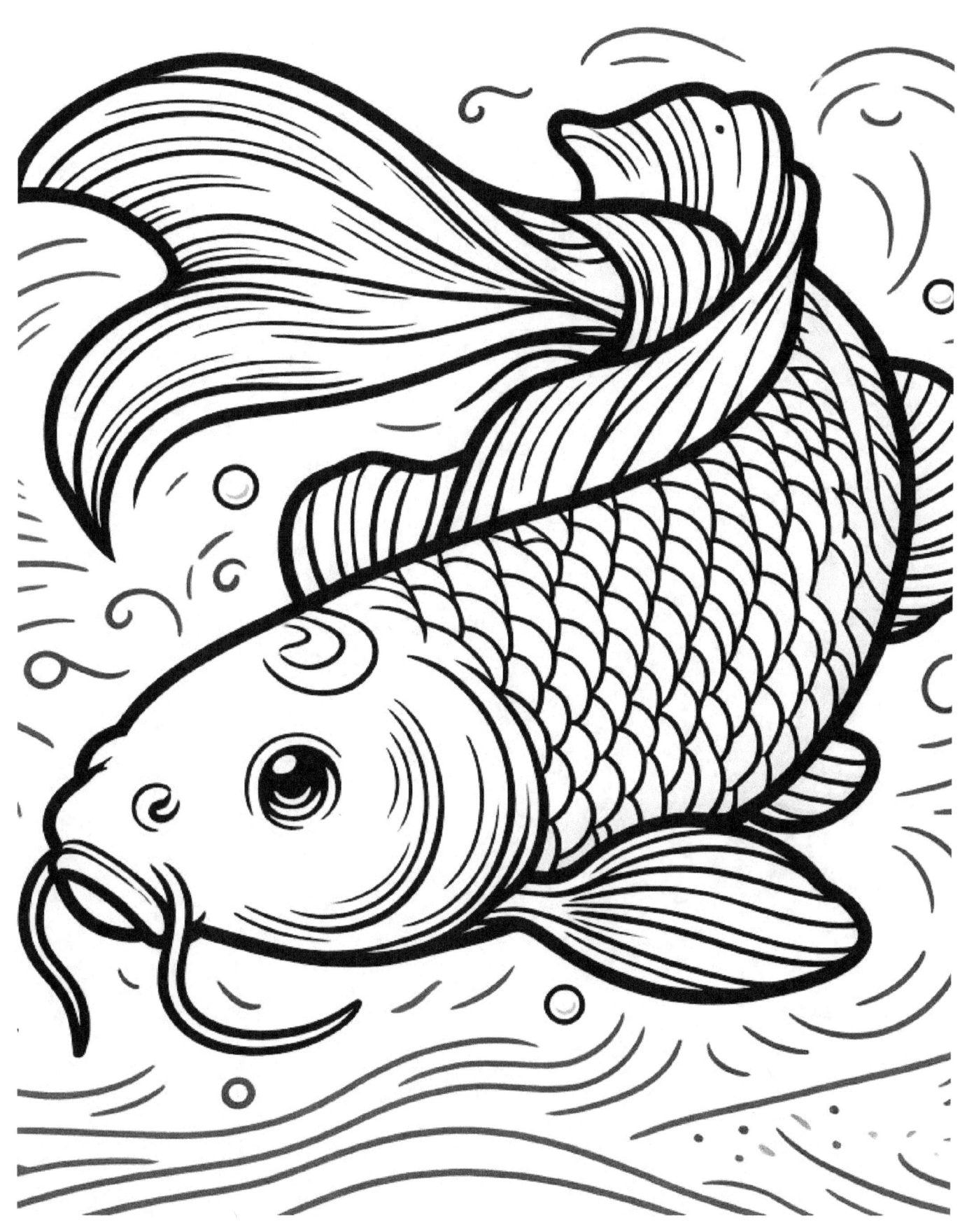

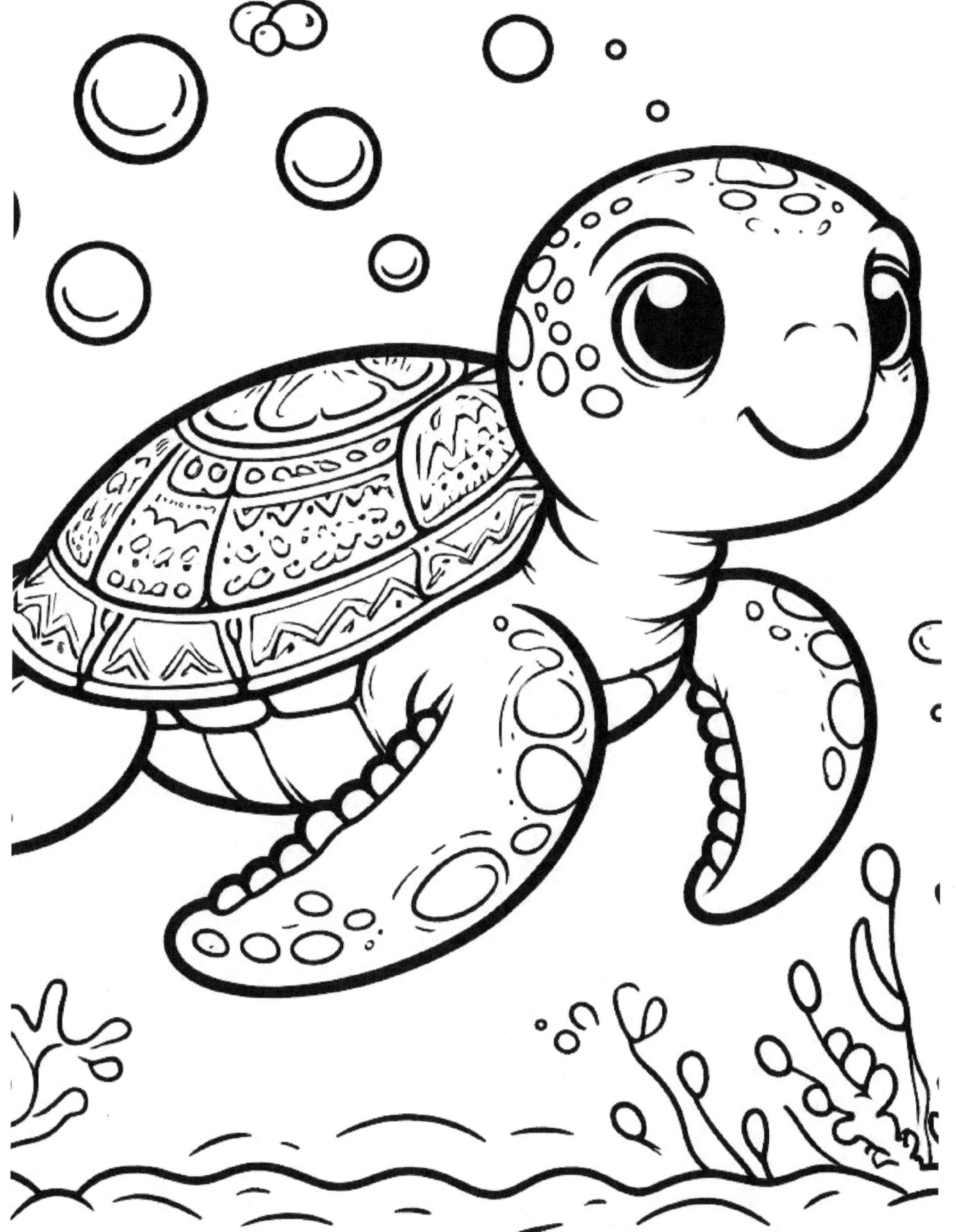

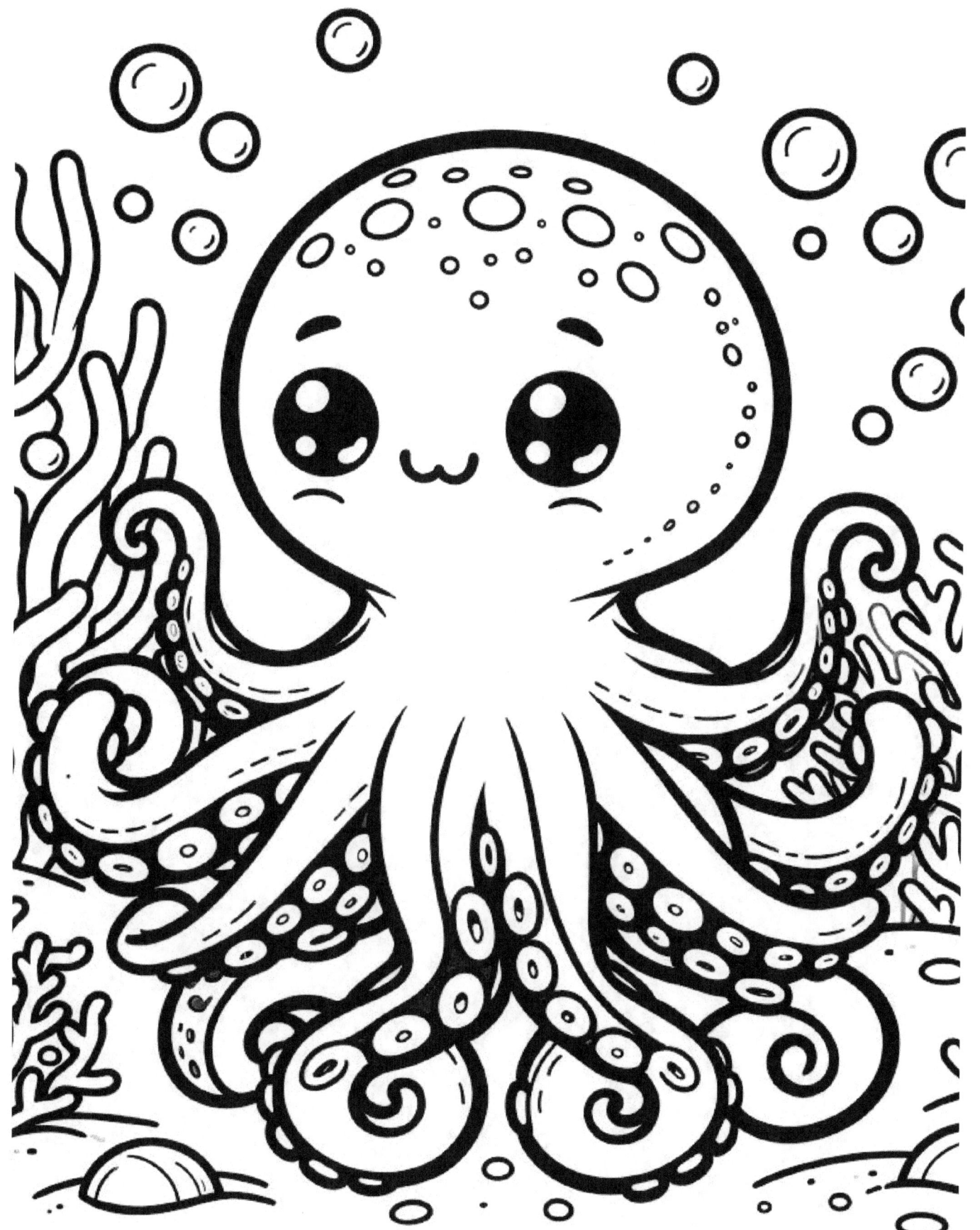

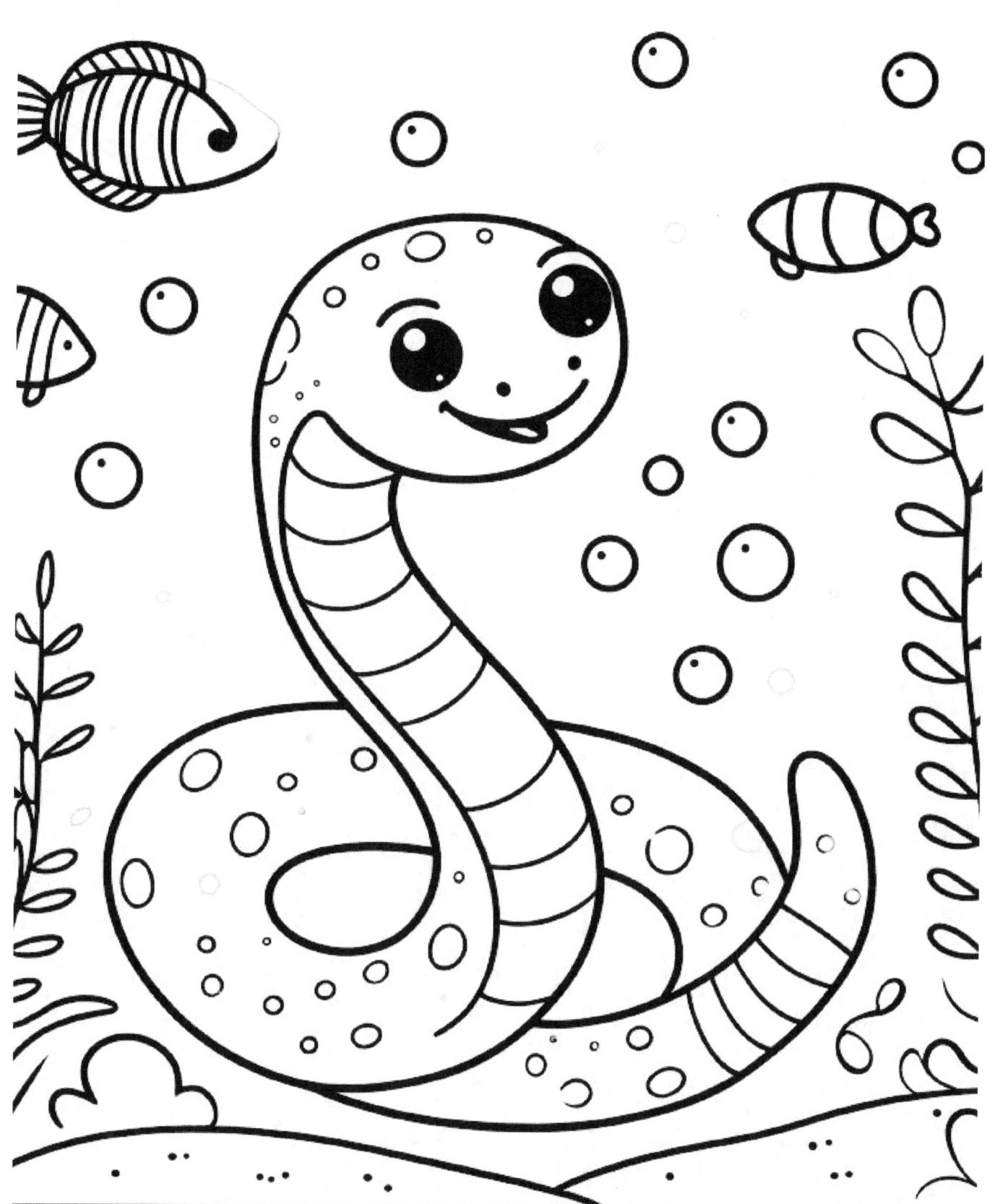

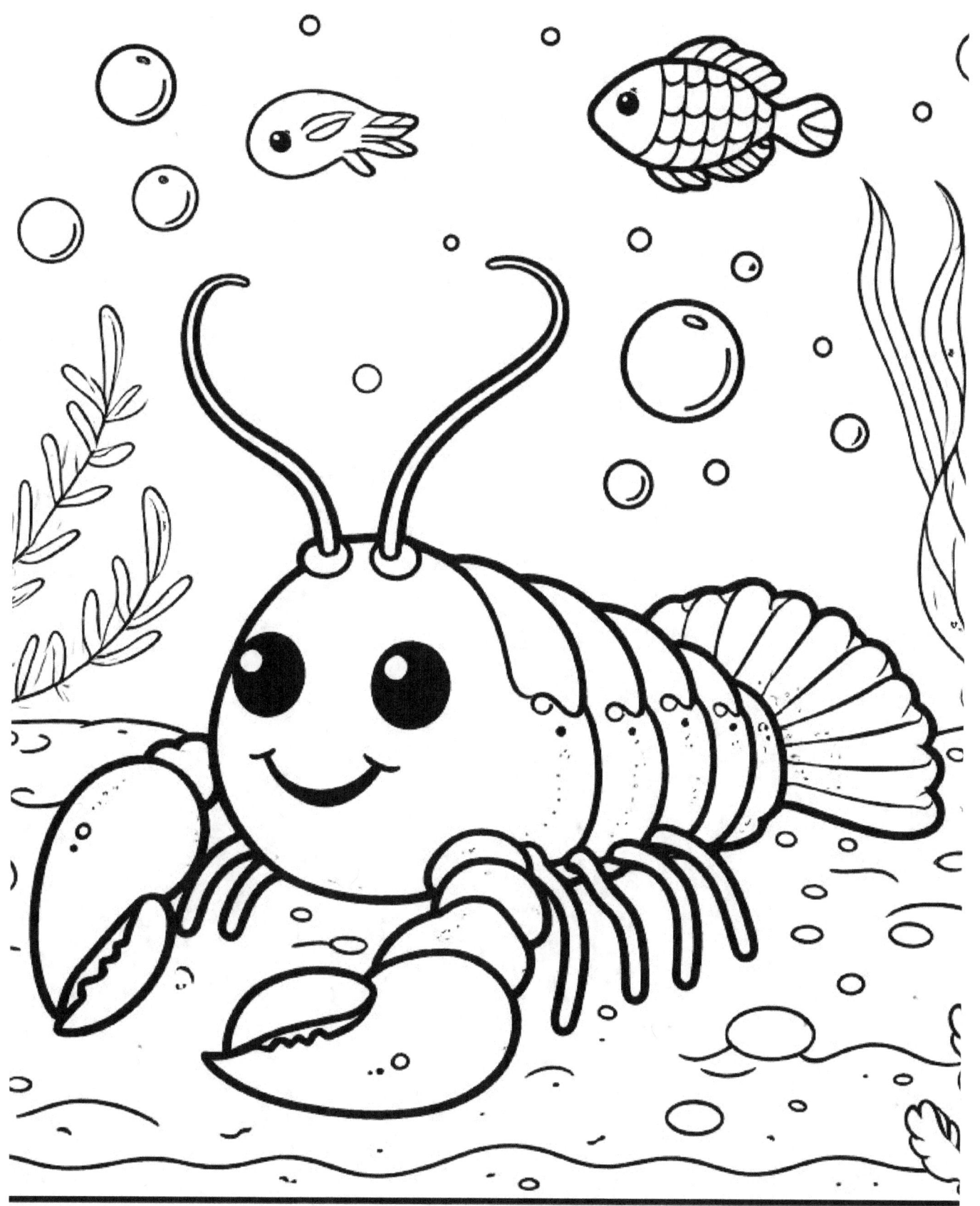

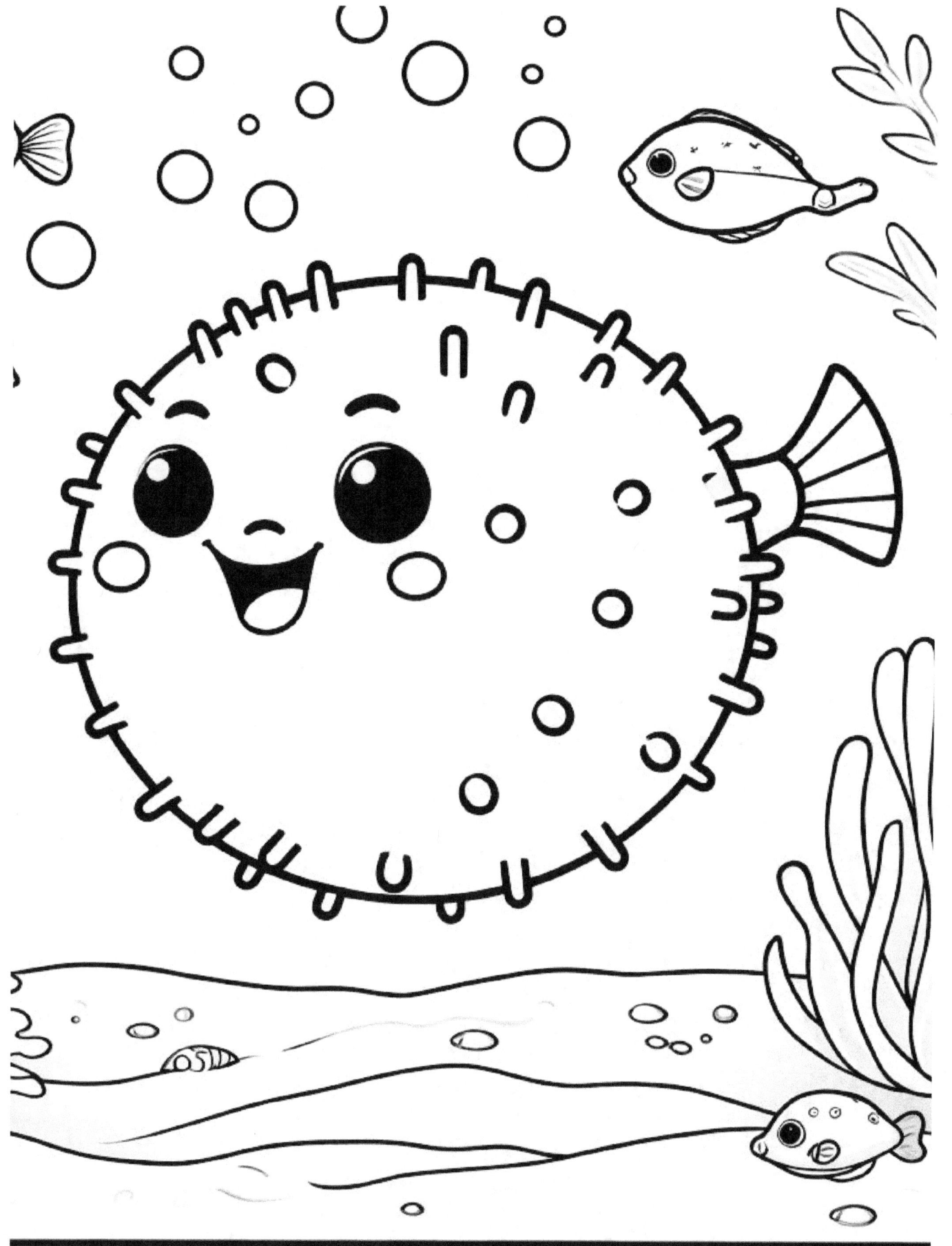

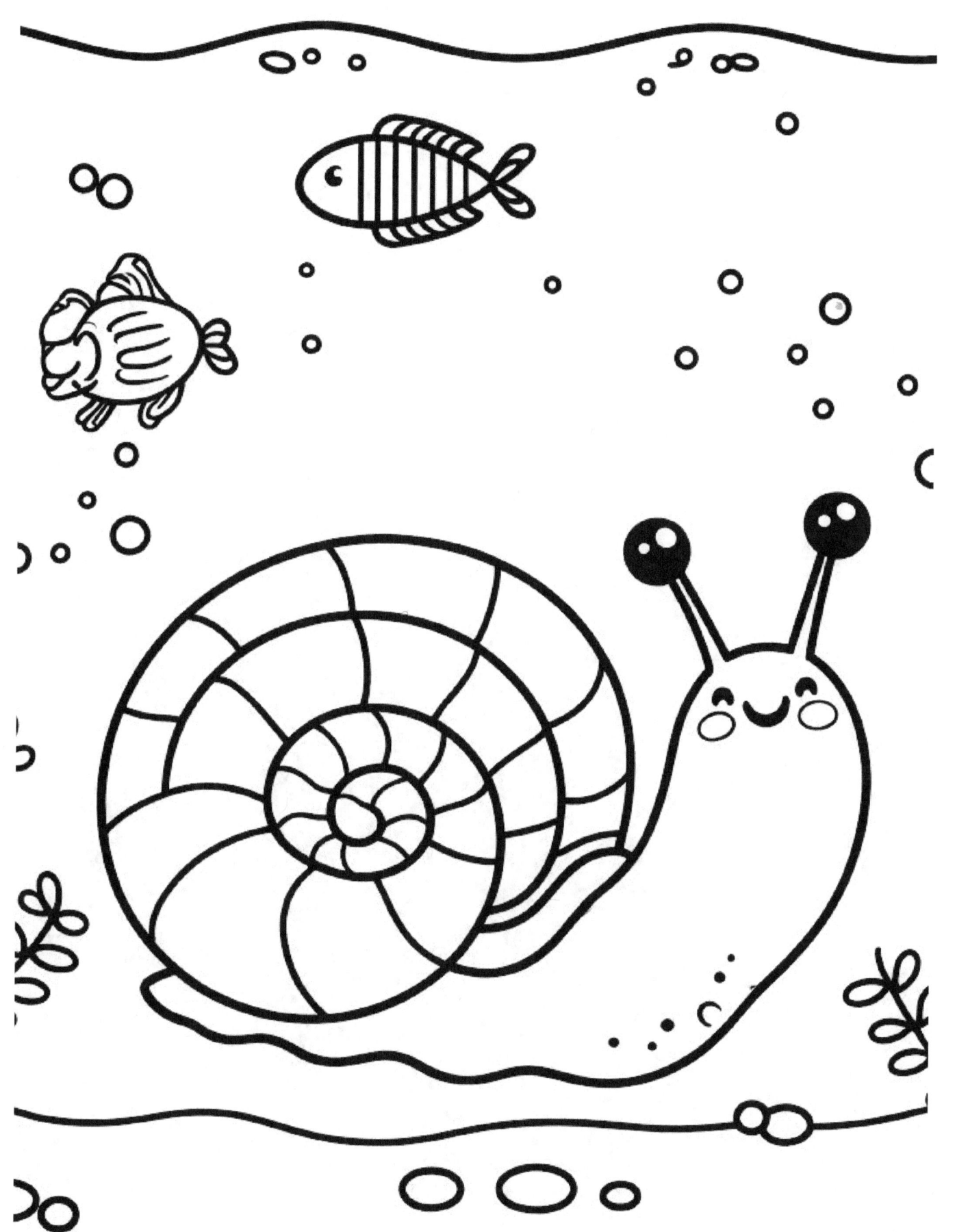

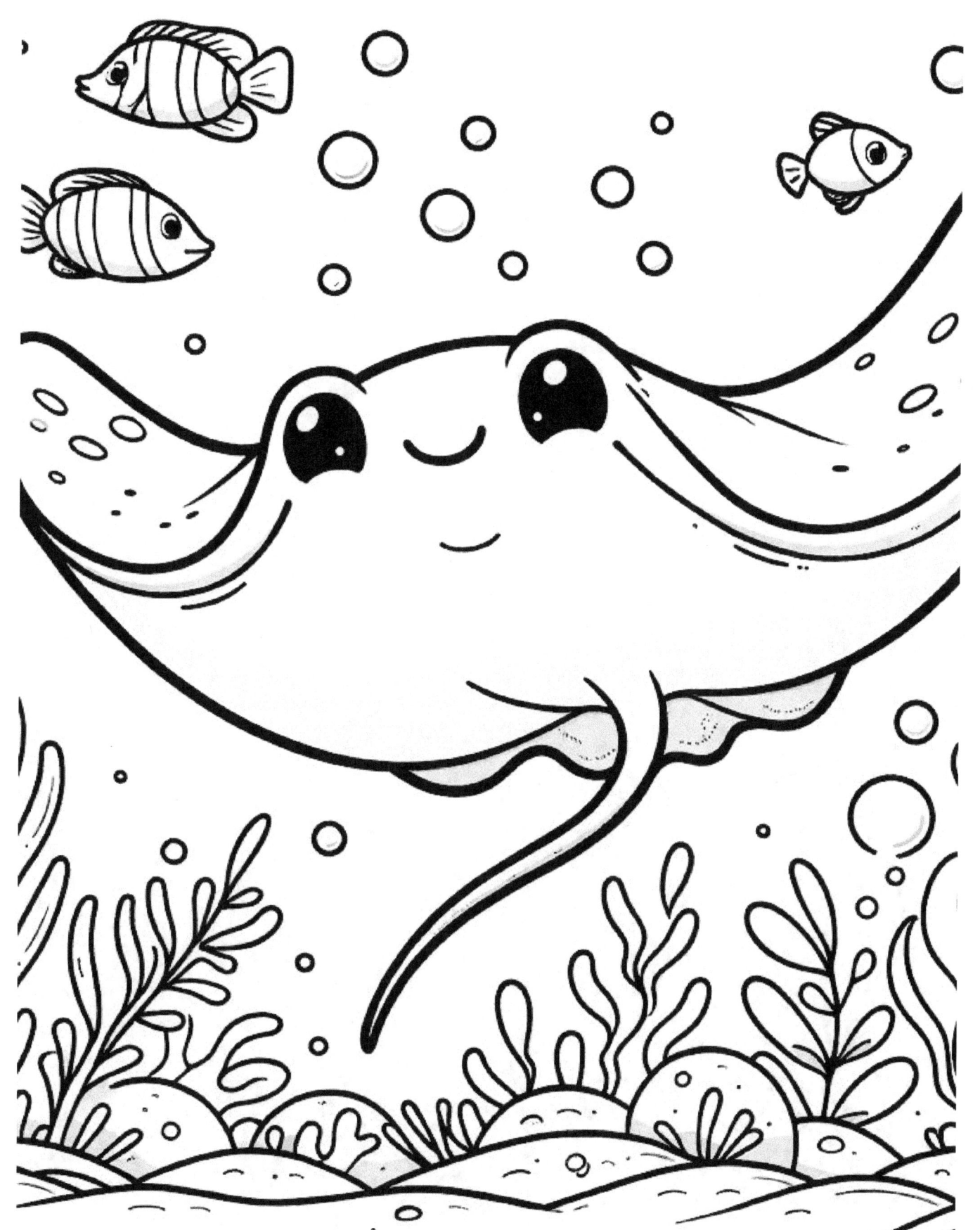

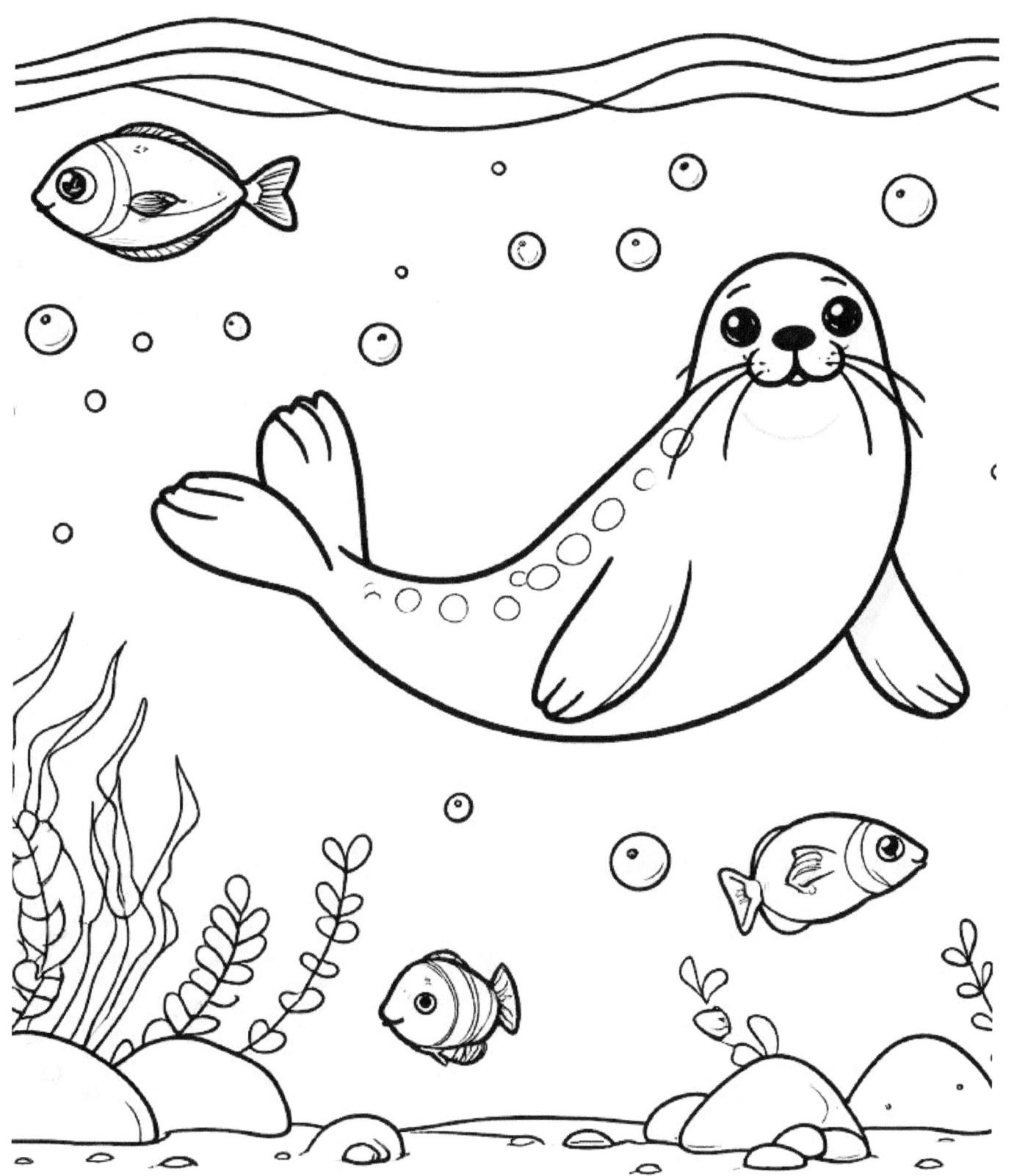

www.ingramcontent.com/pod-product-compliance
Lightning Source LLC
Chambersburg PA
CBHW081436220526
45466CB00008B/2414

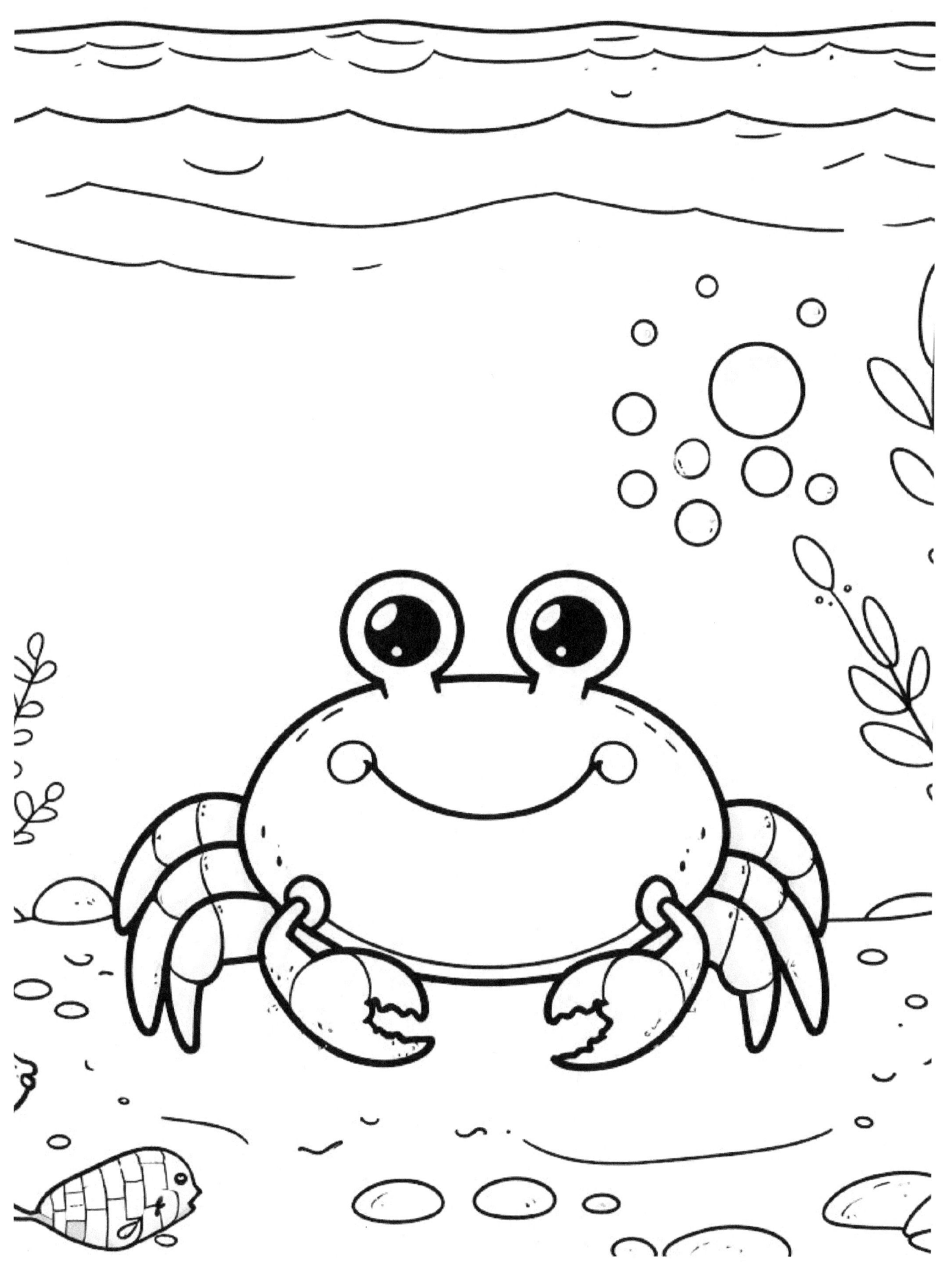

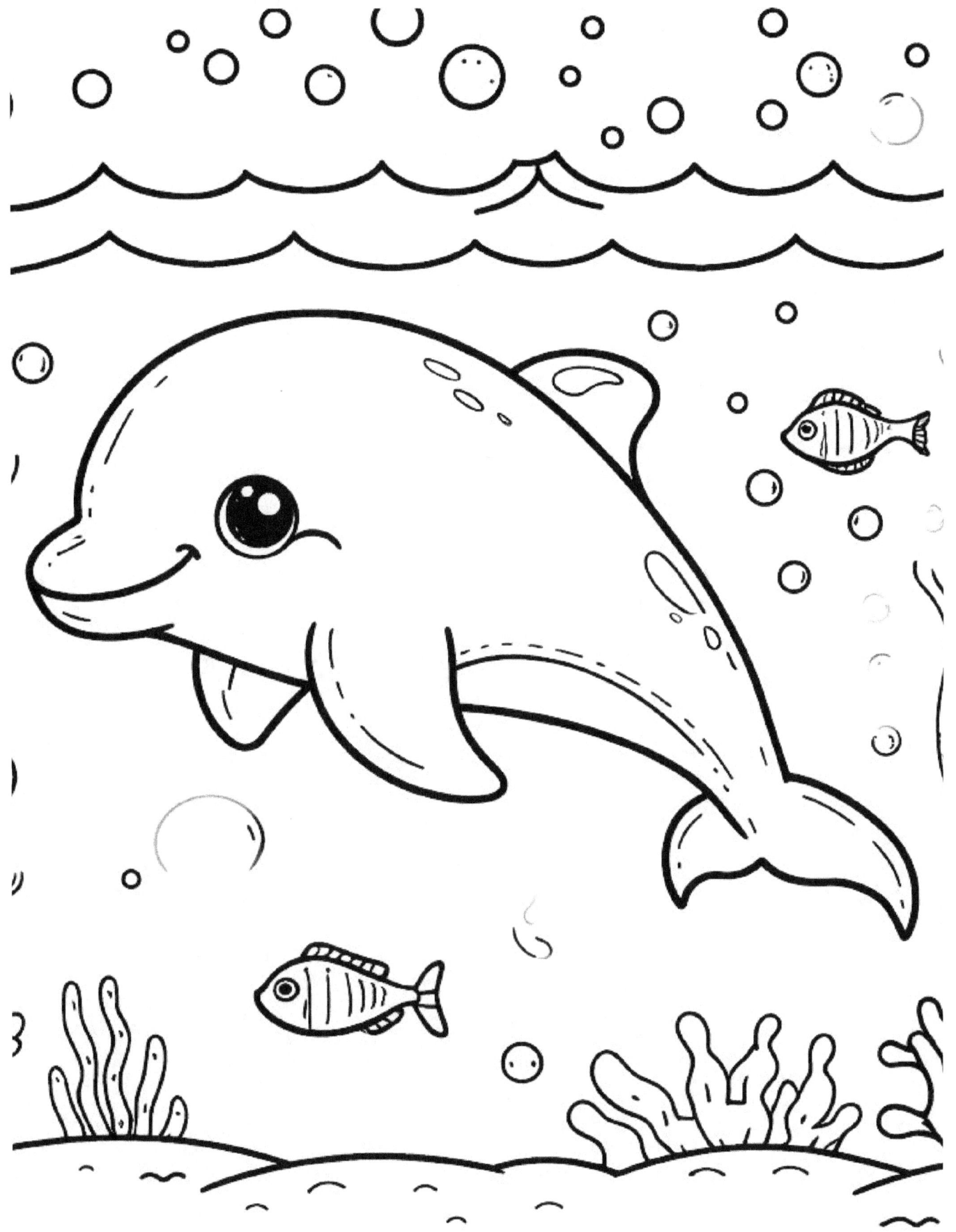

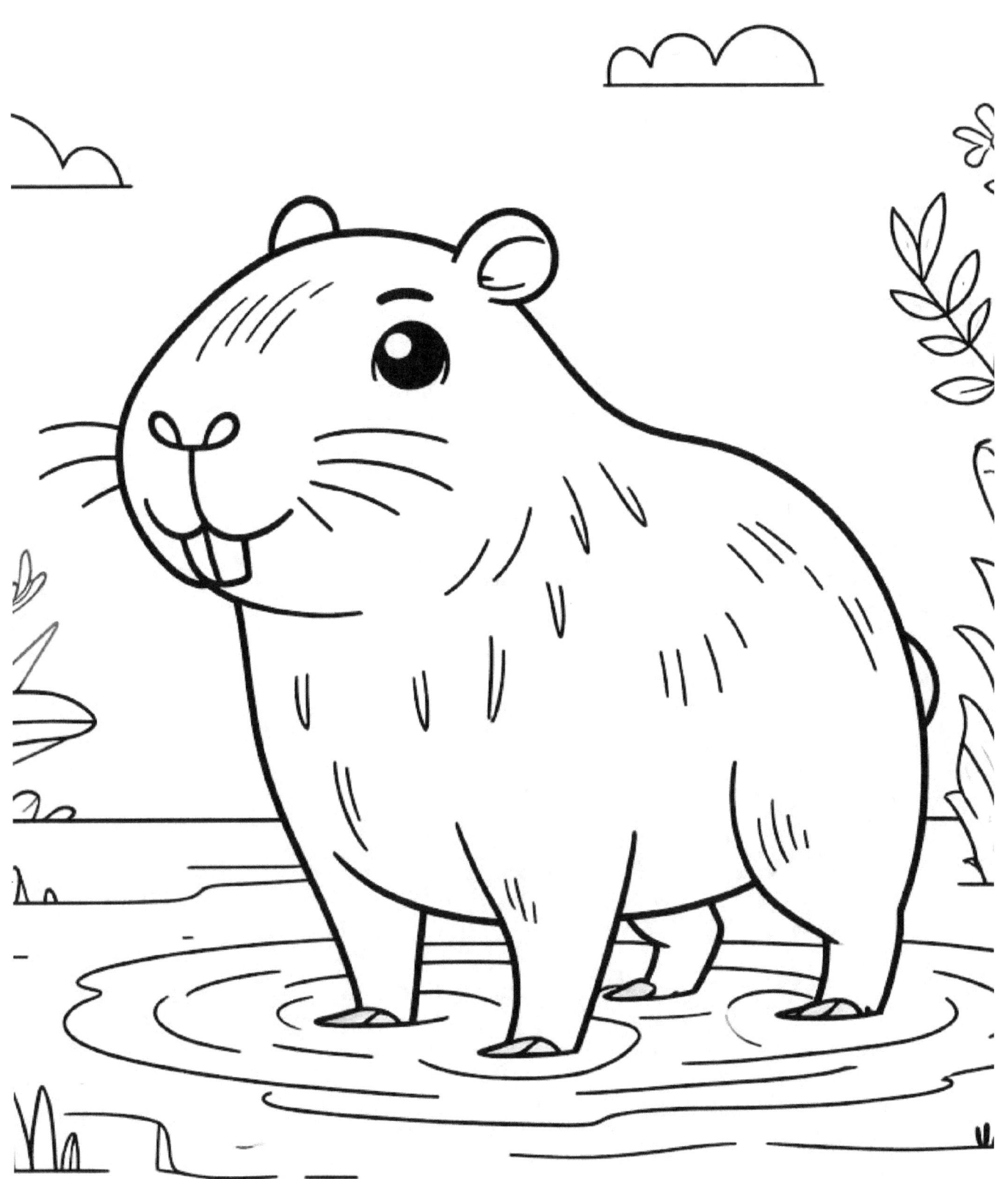

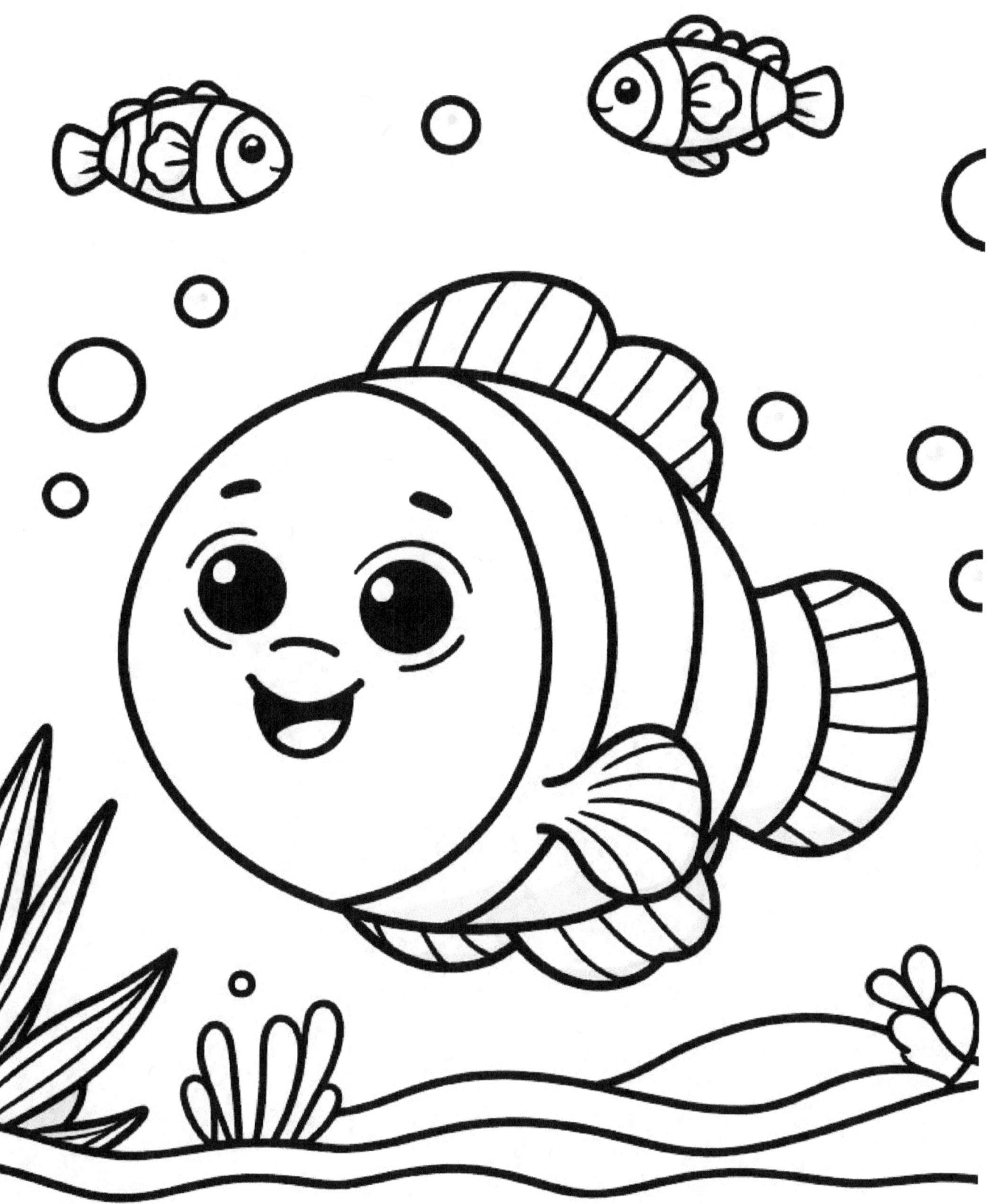

www.ingramcontent.com/pod-product-compliance
Lightning Source LLC
Chambersburg PA
CBHW062157220526
45470CB00009B/2852